Bring the Wu

ADRIENNE VERONESE

Veronese Press

THIS BOOK IS FOR

A.V.

&

B.V.

To become enamored of our powers is to

lose them, at once.

- Lew Welch

Prologue

And the Void said: Let there be pudding;

and there was pudding. Chocolate pudding.

And the Void saw that it was good.

CHAPTER ONE

In the criminal justice system, the people are represented by two separate, yet equally important groups; neither of which is a food group. Nor is either one well known for utilizing pudding in the investigation, apprehension and prosecution of offenders. Not even chocolate pudding. And yet Roz Ferriday found herself asking the question any rational person would upon finding pudding in a cup on her desk yet again: "What is your story?"

The Ventura County Superior Court Bailiff had been finding the mystery pudding in the same spot on her desk every day since the Void started appearing in her courtroom. Not only was it random, it was annoying.

Almost as annoying as the Void.

Roz was not fond of pudding. Especially pudding in a cup. If those being left on her desk were an attempt to get her attention from some secret admirer, that admirer couldn't be very serious in his intentions, since he really hadn't bothered to learn enough about her to know how she felt about pudding. And if they were being left by the Void, there would be hell to pay.

As she swept the latest pudding in a cup off her desk into her wastebasket she took one last look at the visitors in the courtroom. Turning to summon the judge from his chambers, a familiar face in the back of the gallery caught her eye.

Was that a knowing smile on the face of the Void?

Constance Void was the last person on Earth Roz wanted to see in the courtroom. She would rather eat pudding. Every ounce of her was glad it was Thursday. Only one more day before she could hang up the uniform for the weekend, put her tired feet up and work on her knitting.

The Honorable Miguel Gonzales was obviously not in the mood for the look Roz was giving him. It could only mean one thing: the Void was in his courtroom. Again.

"Doesn't that woman have anything better to do with her time?"

She was tempted to answer him, but Roz knew a rhetorical question when she heard it. She was there to tell him the jury had been seated and each witness had arrived. And that was all she was going to tell him.

Almost all, anyway. She'd felt an idea incubating ever since reading the roster that morning and it was about to hatch.

"That guy from the NSA who's coming in to testify that he can't testify was the last one to arrive, your honor; so we're ready for you." She caught her reflection in the mirror behind the judge's desk and tucked a stray hair behind her ear self-consciously before continuing. It was the closest the diminutive bailiff ever came to primping.

"Now that's one sharp dressed man right there, if you ask me. You should see his shoes."

Roz had learned at a young age a man's shoes were directly related to his sense of honor, having heard often of her mother's family crest. As the story goes, Shuman was a name given to cobblers tracing back to the Middle Ages when people were first adopting surnames. Shuman quickly became associated with those of noble character.

Of course, this had nothing to do with whether one

was of noble blood or not because some things never change. The more nobility in a man's blood, the more likely it is his character is entirely suspect.

The true Shuman was of the working class, the salt of the earth laborer who actually knew what a day's work was like and understood the nature of honor and its necessity in any civilized society. Since cobblers took such pride in their work, they tended to make the most durable, finely crafted shoes for themselves. Hence Roz's fascination with a man's shoes. She firmly believed it said something about his character.

"But I didn't ask you."

Judge Gonzales was beginning to speak through clenched teeth. Roz could tell he was already growing impatient. It was never a good sign when it started this early in the day.

"And who gives a damn about his shoes? His being here is nothing but a waste of the court's time, shoes and all."

Roz had long since learned when His Honor spoke of "the court" he was talking about himself. And if there was anything Miguel Gonzales disliked, it was someone wasting his time, which was why she quickly mentioned the other witness who was there to testify.

"That Shill woman is here, too."

Even though the prosecuting attorney had filed a motion to suppress her testimony, Suzanne Shill still clung to the hope the court would rule against him, which they both knew wasn't going to happen.

"You know, your honor, she's got me thinking. There may be a way to take care of our problem with the Void."

Thinking was something he ordinarily discouraged in any of the women in his life, but even Miguel Gonzales had to admit Roz did, on occasion, come up with some pretty good ideas when he permitted her to speak her mind. And if there was even a chance she might have an idea that would get rid of Constance Void, he was willing to hear her out.

Suzanne Shill seemed to have made a career out of giving expert testimony to the court, despite the fact she was only a licensed marriage and family therapist with little more than a master's degree in psychology.

Juries liked her. They liked her neatly pinned hair in its classic French bun and her Laura Ashley print dresses with matching sensible pumps. They liked that she was able to explain things simply and made difficult to grasp concepts easy for them to understand. On more than one occasion, she had provided testimony for a client Judge Gonzales had assigned to her for court-appointed therapy, and therein lay the idea Roz had come up with.

"All you have to do, sir, is find the Void guilty of contempt. Which won't be hard to do because you've warned her more times than I can count if she shows up in your courtroom again that's exactly what you would do. Once you've done that, you can hand her over to Suzanne Shill for court appointed therapy in lieu of jail time. We all know how much Shill loves to convince her patients they need to be in the psych ward. I guarantee you she'll have that Void woman locked up in no time. Voluntarily. Problem solved."

It seemed to Roz the judge was more cheerful than usual as he slipped into his robe and left his chambers. She was fairly certain it was because he was finally going to get rid of Constance Void. But not before a disturbing issue involving badly behaved midgets came to not just their attention, but that of the NSA.

Agent Toole wasn't there to testify, which was no surprise to anyone. But he appreciated the opportunity to get out of his cubicle and see what people looked like in person rather than in bits. The NSA data analyst had been immersed in meta-data about people for so long he had begun to lose touch with what actually made people human.

So it came as no surprise he was startled by the fact the woman seated next to him in the courtroom was actually breathing. Toole had only ever heard people breathing when he listened to their recorded telephone calls and wasn't entirely sure it was something people actually did around each other in person.

And he was fascinated by the woman's furious scribbling of what appeared to be words in the lined yellow notepad she balanced on her knees. Toole hadn't seen anyone write words in longhand since he left grade school. He was lost in a daydream of placing the woman in a museum behind glass where he could display his find to the world when she abruptly turned to him.

"Stop it. You're creeping me out. I bet that's your name, isn't it?"

She leaned into Toole's face. Her unnerving gaze became ground penetrating radar, searching for bodies buried behind his corneas.

"Your name is Creepy Guy."

The eye contact was making him light-headed. So was feeling her breath on his face.

"I'm right, aren't I?"

Toole was so startled by the unexpected sounds coming out of Constance Void's mouth and the feel of her breath, he was speechless.

Words? Were those actual words coming out of the

mouth of a real live breathing person?

He was so beside himself he had to glance at the open bench seat next to him to be sure he wasn't actually sitting next to himself laughing at what an idiot he was being. Since passing an advanced course in suspension of disbelief with perfect marks is something the intelligence industry requires of all its members, Toole was fully expecting to find himself actually sitting there.

Before he could collect himself enough to say anything to the enigmatic scribbler, a pretty bailiff announced the arrival of the presiding judge, asking all to rise as he approached the bench. Because he assumed the reason the woman next to him didn't stand up was she hadn't heard the bailiff, Toole nudged her to get her attention away from the yellow notepad.

"The order to rise doesn't apply to me."

Toole couldn't be certain, but it sounded to him like she was hissing.

"It's only for people who actually respect judges, and I'm not one of those people. Those people are sheep. They seem to ignore the fact that before you can become a judge, you have to be a lawyer. What the fuck is there to respect about lawyers? A judge is nothing more than a lawyer in a fancy robe. And robes invariably make a man vulnerable to corruption."

Toole didn't know what shocked him more, the fact there was more common sense in what the woman had just said than he was used to hearing from anyone, or the fact that the word *fuck* had come out of her mouth. He had heard the word spoken by both men and women equally, but never in real life, never where he could see the word fall from their lips like just so much code weighted by the gravity of the situation.

Toole returned to his seat as the bailiff began to read from the docket while two marshals ushered in a man wearing an orange jumpsuit with his hands cuffed and his legs shackled.

As the judge read the laundry list of charges and asked him how he pleaded, Toole thought of all the times he'd watched the same kiddie porn over the cyber shoulder of some pervert on whose internet line his agency had placed an intercept. It was always the same porn and always the same intercept that re-routed their internet connection to an entirely fictitious internet created and hosted by the NSA. And it invariably resulted in arrests like this pervert's.

The Agency liked to call it *Shooting Fish in a Barrel*. Whether it was due to some sick gratification they got out of it, or simply the curiosity that often stems from unresolved childhood trauma, Toole considered every one of those fish to be getting what they deserved when they turned the information over to local law enforcement. Building a district attorney's career took a certain amount of parallel construction, and the NSA was more than happy to provide the necessary materials.

Somewhere a parallel construction worker is on his analyst's couch exploring the source of his morbid fear of gymnastics. The analyst will never quite grasp that parallel construction workers are phobic of not just uneven parallel bars, but anything that doesn't line up perfectly.

Which is a paradox, since parallel construction requires a great deal of flexibility, especially with things like facts and interpretation of the law.

The rule of thumb is to consider who will profit most from that interpretation. After all, what good is circumventing the Fourth Amendment if stockholders and their political pets can't profit from it?

The thing that surprised him about this defendant was his awareness of the third party intercept on his line. And that was only because some newbie tech working for his internet service provider told him about it when he called to report a problem with his service.

As Toole sat in his cubicle listening through his headphones to the pimple faced geek's voice crack in his adolescent attempt to explain he'd just discovered a third party intercept on the suspect's line, the agent knew their cover had been blown and he'd have to get local law enforcement to move in on the target much sooner than planned. It was the only time he found his work on *Project Barrel Fish* to be less than satisfying.

His attorney had filed a motion to suppress all of the most damning evidence against his client on the grounds the intercept constituted entrapment and was a violation of his Fourth Amendment rights against unlawful search and seizure.

Toole had been subpoenaed to testify about that intercept, but because it would compromise national security to admit the NSA had been involved in any way, or even to admit such technology was being used against the American people, the Agency had filed a motion to suppress the motion to suppress. In the end, the judge had ruled Toole needed to testify, even if it was just to plead the Fifth on behalf of the federal government and not really testify about anything at all.

The fact there was a pony drive upon which the defendant stored the porn he had downloaded was enough to convict him of duplicating, manufacturing, and distributing child pornography anyway, so Toole hadn't been too concerned one of his *Barrel Fish* would get away. Another prison cell would have its occupant, another investor in the prison industrial complex would have his dividends, another Walmart would have its discount goods manufactured by cheap prison labor, and another law enforcement officer would have a notch in his nightstick.

And of course, another District Attorney would have the credits he needed to feed the political machine the NSA so dearly loved to prop up. Justice would be served, unless of course the expert who was asked to testify about the defendant's mental health was allowed on the witness stand.

The last thing the NSA needed was a single case to be lost due to mitigating factors like an abusive childhood, and the suggestion therapy would be a better course of action than a prison sentence. That's just not the kind of nonsense the NSA could get behind. This was America, after all.

Although he was pleased the prosecutor had selected a sufficiently computer illiterate jury, it meant everything about the evidence against the defendant had to be spelled out in crayon. As he sat through the long boring hours of dry testimony about torrent files, default settings and the difference between upload and download, his attention kept wandering to the fascinating scribblings of the woman seated next to him. She was making no effort to conceal what she wrote. Toole's curiosity was more than piqued by one of the words she'd neatly printed at the very top of the page and then made bold by tracing over again and again with her ball point pen: **Alliance**.

Alliances were something members of the intelligence community were always on the lookout for. As any good citizen in post 9-11 America should be.

When alliances formed, it was almost always a sign something was out of control, since it was the agenda of the intelligence industry to do everything in its power to prevent people from finding common ground. Coming together in agreement was not something the American government wanted to encourage its people to do. In fact, Congress prided itself in providing a role model for how to avoid it at all cost.

On more than one occasion Constance Void noticed Roz, her favorite bailiff in Ventura County Superior Court, sneaking a surreptitious glance at the sharp dressed man seated next to her. Roz was the reason Constance came into this courtroom.

The Void loved nothing more than to share with Roz the inspirations that came to her as she sat in the highly polished wooden pews so generously provided by the people of Ventura County. Her inspiration this day had come entirely from the judge's robe and the juror with dreadlocks he scolded for wearing board shorts into his courtroom.

Despite their obvious differences, Constance Void couldn't help but feel she and Roz were kindred spirits. Both had served their communities in unorthodox ways. Both had gone unappreciated by those communities, as though they were invisible to them. And both were surprisingly adept at dealing with men in positions of power. Which was why it came as no surprise to her Roz kept glancing in the direction of the man sitting next to her.

Yes, he was a creepy guy, but she sensed he meant well. From the way he was dressed Constance suspected he was a member of the intelligence community. And from what she'd gathered about the case being tried and the experts being called to testify, she had to conclude Creepy Guy was with the NSA.

Not my cup of tea, but Roz does deserve someone who knows how to navigate the fashion industry.

She couldn't help but sense a kind of déjà vu about the situation though, having seen Roz helplessly apply her nonexistent flirting skills on various well-dressed professionals enough times to know they just didn't work.

As she finished up her latest creation for the

amusement of her favorite bailiff and the morning's proceedings drew to a close, she thought about how she might facilitate the coming together of the splendid Miss Roz Ferriday and the sharp dressed creepy guy.

Judge Gonzales banged his gavel listlessly as he announced lunch recess and ordered the jury to return in ninety minutes. Impulsively, Constance tore her story out of the notepad and hastily folded it before turning to Agent Toole.

"Do me a favor?" she said, thrusting the story into his hand. "Give this to the bailiff. I have somewhere I need to be and can't hang around waiting to get her attention."

With that, Constance Void rushed from the courtroom and sprinted for the restroom down the hall because it was not in her to tell a lie. She really did have somewhere she needed to be. But of course it had much more to do with the TrainWreck than it did with anything else one would ordinarily do in a ladies' room.

If he was anything, Agent Toole was a man who knew how to think on his feet. Pulling his cell phone out of his pocket, he sat back down and smoothed the document out on the bench seat next to him, taking several snapshots of the data written on the front and back before refolding it and making his way to the bailiff's desk.

"Excuse me."

Roz pretended not to notice him standing there. Toole failed to notice Roz pretending not to notice him because the oddly out of place pudding cup perched on the edge of her desk distracted him. It was chocolate. He didn't know why, but the stellar field agent in him told the data analyst in him it was significant. Holding the folded yellow paper out to her, he gave the pretty bailiff an awkward smile.

"There was a woman sitting next to me in the back, and she asked me to give you this. I guess she had to leave."

Roz scowled when she recognized the childish scrawl of the Void. His Honor hadn't wanted to disrupt the morning's proceedings with the plan they had devised for dumping their problematic courtroom visitor on Suzanne Shill. The perfectly coiffed licensed marriage and family therapist had stopped by her desk to assure Roz before she left for lunch she would be back for the rest of that day's proceedings, but Roz had no idea whether the Void would be returning.

"Did she say whether she would be back?"

"No, she didn't."

Ever the observant one, the data analyst in him noted the golden flecks in the bailiff's hazel eyes forming a halo around her irises. "She left before I got the chance to speak with her. I'd wanted to ask her where I could get a decent lunch nearby."

Sensing the NSA agent was a man in possession of a certain amount of power, Roz played her cards the only way she knew how to, given the situation. Smiling, she insisted he join her for lunch in the downstairs cafeteria where she could show him exactly what to order and what not to.

"Best kept secret in all of Ventura County."

Dropping the folded note from Constance Void into the top drawer of her desk, she locked it and absently swept the cup of pudding into the wastebasket with her forearm.

"Not a fan of pudding?"

"Not really. And I wish I knew who keeps leaving it on my desk."

Exiting the courtroom with the handsome NSA agent, Roz found herself unable to take her eyes off his shoes. Toole tried to make light banter as they rode the elevator to the lower level of the courthouse, but light banter had never been his strong suit. It was the kind of thing a person needed to have practice at to get right, and Toole just didn't spend enough time out of his cubicle to get much practice at anything involving real breathing people who made actual words come out of their mouths. It was made even more difficult by his forced suppression of the question he really wanted to ask Roz.

"Are you wondering what that thing was the Void wrote me?" Roz slid into the seat across from him at the only open table they were able to find. "I can only imagine a man in your line of work would be intrigued; am I right?"

Toole was surprised to find his lunch date so adept at putting him at ease while simultaneously seeming to be telepathic. Nodding, he pointed to his mouth full of California roll dipped in Thai peanut sauce, hoping she'd understand why he didn't reply.

"Constance Void has been coming into our courtroom for over a year now. And for some reason, she's got it in her head she and I have something in common. She sits in the gallery and writes these ridiculous stories she always dedicates to me. Stoner riffs, she calls them. Frankly, I can't make heads or tails of them and can't for the life-of-me figure out what she thinks I'm getting out of it."

Toole couldn't help but think Roz had the woman all wrong. From what he'd observed, she was highly intelligent and seemed to know exactly what she was doing. That she was submitting written material directly to the court told him she had access to information she needed to get to someone working inside the judicial system. That someone was without a doubt a government employee, which made the situation even more worrisome. And the fact a professional like Roz couldn't understand any of it told him Constance Void was writing in code.

"Does she tell you to pass these riffs along to anyone else, or explain what she's doing in your courtroom?" Roz nodded and delicately wiped her mouth with the napkin from her lap before answering.

"She insists they're *for the record.*"

She said it with air quotes and a shrug. "As for what she's doing there, she's fond of telling the guards at the entrance she's our court *steganographer.* Not stenographer. *Steganographer.* What does that even mean?"

Agent Toole knew exactly what that meant. His hunch about Constance Void had been right all along. She was writing in code, and someone in the court system, someone working for the government, was the recipient.

The thing about steganography was it could be staring you right in the face, hanging out on the street corner for all to see like some thuggie's underwear. But unless you knew it was a code, and knew the key, you would never even recognize it as something other than the crack of that thuggie's ass. Only the sender and the recipient would have the vaguest idea how to break the code because of how specific to each party it could be. And the one she had just given Roz had to do with an alliance.

Suspecting he had stumbled upon something that might threaten national security, the sharp dressed NSA agent excused himself and went to the restroom where he could sit in the privacy of a stall and read the document on his smart phone.

THE ALLIANCE OF THE SIXTEEN
BADLY BEHAVED JEWISH MIDGETS
a stoner riff for Roz

I got an email from my girlfriend Sadie the other day. Sadie's no poser. She's a Gangster Old School for sure, but more of a supermodel Gangster, with no discernible evidence that she has ever eaten. She's a tough chick, and street smart. But she has no idea what she's gotten herself into.

She told me she was working as a "continental" hostess at a fine hotel, which made me suspicious immediately. What continent needs its own hostess? Seemed fishy to me.

My hunch was confirmed when she told me she

was required by her employer to babysit sixteen little Jews. The only little Jews I know of who behave so badly they require babysitting in fine hotels, even Southern California hotels, have been spread around the world being watched carefully for decades. All sixteen of them.

It seemed highly unlikely, but I checked that passage in Technicians of the Sacred once again, and did a little snooping on the internet. My heart chilled in the ninety degree heat. It had happened.

Worse than the League of Extraordinary Midgets, who almost took down Hollywood, the sixteen Badly Behaved Jewish Midgets had formed an Alliance.

No man in a robe or wide cut board shorts would be safe. Catholic churches would be targeted first of course, and then...the Rastafarians!!! Oh my gawd those sweet gentle souls! They needed to be warned immediately. I fired up my bong and began sending smoke signals.

Om Shiva Shanka, Hare Hare Ganja filled the air as I paced the floor, chanting fervently for the protection of their foreskins.

I honestly did not know what to do. I fired off some more smoke signals to the Rastafarians and thought carefully about what I needed to tell Sadie. If she knew what those filthy midget Jews were up to, she'd get her peeps and go and represent and there would be a war. Rampart would show up, somebody with a cell phone would record it, and the entire thing would be dismissed as inadmissible. Another gang injunction would be placed on Oxnard, and then Las Colonias would get into it. Sheer hell from there on out. For sure.

I wrote Sadie and insisted she find a job at a more reputable establishment, remove the lip rings, and meet some nice gentleman of good breeding. With her looks, she'll end up in Bel Air in no time. Everybody is circumcised there. She'll never even know what those sixteen little Jews were up to.

(Disclaimer: this riff is not intended in any way to slander, profile, impugn, discredit, dog out, or in any way insult badly behaved Jewish midgets. There is a problem with only sixteen specific badly behaved Jewish midgets, and the Rastafarians are taking care of it. The others are probably perfectly nice people. We should support them in their effort to understand why they are so badly behaved.)

Agent Toole could hardly contain himself as he returned to Roz and tried to conceal his excitement.

His discovery could be just the thing he'd hoped for, the thing that would get him out of his cubicle and into an office with a view of downtown Los Angeles. He had been a data analyst long enough to know he was born to be a man of action, and men of action loved nothing more than a great view.

Not only had he discovered intel about an alliance, he'd discovered intel about an international alliance. And because it involved such a large number of Jews, he suspected the Israelis may be involved. Most likely Mossad. This was just the kind of thing the NSA was always looking for to justify getting more funding from Congress.

The thing that made it even more intriguing for Toole was the fact it involved such a lethal group of very small people. He was pretty sure they preferred to be called "little people," but would look it up when he got back to his cubicle. Toole may not have a lot of experience actually interacting with genuine breathing people in real life, but he knew enough to not call little people midgets. That's just plain wrong, even if they were Jewish and very badly behaved.

And then of course there was the issue of Ms. Void's *smoke signals*. If there was even the slightest possibility the woman had come up with some kind of unbreakable code, including a stealth delivery system for it that office with a view could very well be a corner office.

There was nothing that interested the intelligence community more than an unbreakable code. Toole sensed he was on his way to becoming a truly stellar field agent, even though the NSA doesn't have field agents. Toole liked to think of himself as a trailblazer, and had a feeling he was blazing a trail for a whole new field of work for the NSA. Besides, if they didn't intend to have stellar field agents, why on Earth would the NSA have a program called *Stellar Wind?*

He wasn't sure whether to be relieved or nervous when the Void slid back into the seat next to him just after the jury returned from lunch. No sooner had Roz announced the Honorable Justice Miguel Gonzales and he'd taken his seat at the bench than two things happened at once: Agent Toole realized he would never again be able to look at a man in a robe without glancing around nervously for very short people holding sharp objects, and the distinct click-click-click of sensible pumps slapped the linoleum tiles as Suzanne Shill made her perfectly color-coordinated entrance fashionably late.

"Ah, Mizz Shill, just the person I was hoping to see."

The judge waved her up to the bench cheerfully. As she approached, Roz the curvaceous bailiff joined them and the three spoke quietly without the benefit of listening devices for several minutes, which irritated Toole and made him realize there were some gaps in the NSA's blanket surveillance of everything. Or at least loose threads, which would make this more of a thin thread than a gap. His curiosity was piqued when the woman's back stiffened as she swung around and her skirt ballooned in a Laura Ashley moment of fashionable indignation. Her pumps clicked even more fiercely as she found a seat and set her perfectly color-coordinated laptop case down on the bench next to her.

Judge Gonzales cleared his throat and announced he had ruled with the prosecution and decided the testimony of the LMFT who had worked with the defendant was irrelevant to the case and would not be allowed. Agent Toole sighed in relief.

He knew better than anyone there how easily the case against the *Barrel Fish* defendant could derail with her testimony, having himself seen the grainy footage of the defendant as a young boy circulating on their own network. Nothing irritated the NSA more than someone trying to use the excuse having been a victim of the crime was a valid reason to look at that filth.

He was expecting to see the therapist storm out of the courtroom in a click-click-clicking flurry, but the judge surprised him by demanding Constance Void approach the bench. As the surprised code talker rose and walked noiselessly up the aisle in her worn red Chuck Taylors, the judge read off a list of grievances against her, concluding that he had found her in contempt of court.

"I'm giving you the option of time in jail, or you can undergo six months of court appointed therapy with Suzanne Shill here." The judge nodded toward the licensed marriage and family therapist and Constance glanced at her briefly before speaking. Toole wasn't sure, but he thought he saw her shudder.

"I'm not sure which of the two is worse. How much jail time are we talking about here?"

Toole wondered if the Void knew something about the therapist the others didn't know. More and more, the woman was intriguing him.

"If you choose the jail time, I will also slap a hefty fine on you to cover the costs. Considering how much time you spend in this courtroom, something tells me you don't have the kind of income that could easily cover that expense."

Agent Toole watched the two women leave the courtroom together and wished he could have followed them. But the NSA agent still had to testify that he couldn't testify. And besides, once he got back to his cubicle he had all the tools he needed to put both of them under surveillance. Once he logged on to his terminal and entered the necessary data, there was very little information about either woman he would not be privileged to.

If either woman had a computer system at home, he could clone their monitors remotely using the backdoor key, even if the computers were turned off. And of course putting an intercept on their lines would be a snap. If Suzanne had a camera and microphone in that laptop of hers, he could easily listen in and watch anything in range of it. As well, if Shill was stupid enough to bring her cell phone into the therapy sessions with her, he would be able to listen in on anything the Void might tell her that could lead him to Mossad and those midgets. And maybe those smoke signals too.

Considering he had never functioned as an agent outside his cubicle and had so little experience interacting with actual breathing people, Agent Toole had to admit he really did have what it takes to be a truly stellar field agent, and it wouldn't be long before the NSA had to admit it too.

CHAPTER TWO

The trouble with her new client started right away
when Constance Void made it perfectly clear to
Suzanne Shill she would not be coming into her office
for their therapy sessions. She insisted she had an
irrational fear of visiting any state that doesn't have
medical marijuana, to which the therapist replied that
her office was less than thirty minutes from where
Constance lived, not in another state.

"The Laura Ashley wallpaper and matching throw
pillows in the waiting room confuse me."

"What does my décor have to do with anything?"

"Have you ever been to the State of Confusion?
It's not a medical marijuana state, you know. I find that
uncomfortably arresting. Therefore, I prefer to not go
there."

Suzanne Shill had no idea what that even meant,
but made a note that she thought her client had an
irrational fear of being arrested. Had she shared that

opinion out loud, Constance would have demanded to know who doesn't.

"Besides, I can't enjoy the TrainWreck in your office."

Suzanne made another note to explore the client's fascination with train wrecks and see if it was connected to a deeper pathology involving disasters in general. Yet every time she brought it up, the Void's response was to tell her the smoke signals should make it perfectly obvious.

"In fact, it would be far easier for me to communicate with you via smoke signal. From a distance. Do you provide that kind of service to your clients?"

Suzanne just stared blankly without blinking, unsure if she should even tell the client she sometimes does sessions online. She did eventually agree to working with her over the internet. But she made it clear she expected Constance Void's full cooperation. Instinct told her the Void was one client who needed a short leash. In fact, she wasn't beyond suspecting Constance Void's repeated references to smoke signals could actually be her way of alluding to some kind of secret language. After all, delusional patients are sometimes known to develop them from within more complex delusional systems.

It seemed to her Constance Void was going deeper and deeper into her *court steganographer* delusion. The concern of course was her client may be dissipating into a full blown psychosis. More and more she wondered if Constance might need to be hospitalized.

Hospitalizing clients had become the licensed marriage and family therapist's specialty. She liked to think of it as a badge of honor, a necessary tool of the trade that few had the strength of conviction to fully utilize. Visiting her clients in the hospital was the kind of thing she reserved her best Laura Ashley print dresses and matching pumps for. She liked the distinct sound those pumps made walking down the hallway to her clients' locked rooms. It was soothing. Sometimes the only way she could fall asleep at night was by replaying that sound in her head over and over again.

She was lingering over her third glass of wine that evening pondering her new client's excessive use of the controlled substance God clearly didn't want his perfect yet fallen and therefore entirely sinful children having anything to do with. Perhaps her approach should be to convince the Void she had a substance abuse problem and needed to go into rehab. Suzanne did have admitting privileges at a rehab center. It also took psychiatric patients. She thought it could be perfect for Constance.

She was lost in thought about the possibilities when the phone rang. It startled her at first, in part because she had fallen into a wine-fueled fantasy about the sound of her pumps on institutional linoleum as she walked down that hallway wearing her finest Laura Ashley dress to visit her poor delusional client, and in part because the phone never rang that late at night. Most of her clients had learned late night calls tended to result in a 72 hour stay in a facility with automatic dispensers in every room timed to spray cockroach killer at them every fifteen minutes.

Little did Suzanne Shill know when she finally did reach for the phone it was a call that was to change her life. Had her husband not been working late at the office for the third night in a row, she would have had him answer it, for obvious reasons. Women just can't be too careful these days, and answering the phone late at night was never a safe thing for any woman. Suzanne considered it courting disaster. Even so, there she was, picking up the phone to the voice of Constance Void telling her she was in trouble. She had been picked up by Oxnard Police for associating with known gang members and they told her she would only be released into her court-appointed therapist's custody.

"Why me?"

Suzanne repeated the self-esteem life raft mantra for the chronically deflated ego while pointlessly clinging to the hope it might keep her from sinking any further into the gloom of another lost evening. The jail was in a part of Oxnard she preferred to not even know existed. And the parking facility made her feel dirty. To make matters worse, there was a car idling in the shadows with two creepy looking Asian men sitting in it watching her. It was almost more than she could bear. As if that wasn't enough, she learned too late it didn't matter that she was there as an officer of the court, she still had to undergo the humiliation of a thorough security screening. They actually made her remove the bobby pins from her hair.

What do they think I'm going to do with them?

As she walked down the hall to where Constance was being held the staccato click-click-clicking of her pumps spelled out her indignation in a code that didn't take a cryptographer to crack. Because Suzanne believed her power as a woman was centered entirely in her hair, the fact that it now had no bobby pins keeping it in place made her feel less than powerful. In fact, Suzanne Shill felt disturbingly vulnerable.

The two women didn't speak until they got to Suzanne's car. Much to her disappointment, the first words out of Constance Void's mouth had nothing to do with her recent incarceration. They were about the upholstery.

"What kind of freak gets upholstery for their car that matches their office décor?"

The question set the tone for how the rest of the discussion would be going, and although Suzanne tried valiantly to correct the course they were on, it was to no avail.

"Do you really think that is more important than you explaining to me what you were doing associating with known gang members in that part of Oxnard?"

She was trying to give Constance the steeliest gaze she was capable of, but it wasn't easy. By that time of night her mascara had mostly flaked off and left smeared smudge marks under her eyes. Suzanne Shill would tell you in no uncertain terms giving anyone a steely gaze with flaked, smudged mascara is dubious – at best.

"Don't be ridiculous."

Constance rolled her eyes and explained they weren't Oxnard gang members, they were Chinese. "Everyone knows Oxnard doesn't have any Chinese gang members. These guys were up from Los Angeles to bring me what I thought were the rare herbs I needed for a potion I'm working on."

"I don't really care where they were from."

Suzanne felt herself growing angry. She hadn't really eaten anything but a few slices of cheese and some water crackers with her wine, and her blood sugar was starting to dip.

"The fact remains, Oxnard Police identified them as members of a street gang and because you are under orders from the court to not associate with any criminal element, they picked you up." She was trying to get her client to see she had done this to herself, that by her own actions she had put herself in a situation that required a person of trust to get her out.

But it was obvious Constance wasn't listening. Her attention had been focused entirely on something she was seeing in the passenger side mirror since they first pulled out of the parking lot at the Oxnard Police Department. At some point after the stoplight at Rose Avenue, she gripped Suzanne's upper arm and told her to take the next left.

"And whatever you do, act natural. Don't look behind you. We don't want them to know we've spotted them."

Constance Void was speaking with both a seriousness and an urgency that seemed unlike her, and it startled Suzanne.

She took the turn before she really had time to consider that a delusional woman was telling her someone was following them. And of course she noticed someone behind them, they were in traffic. *There's always someone behind someone else on Rose Avenue.* But something about that urgency in her client's voice told Suzanne to do what Constance Void was telling her.

She pulled into the parking lot of the Krispy Kreme, but kept the car in gear and left the engine running exactly as Constance instructed. And much to her distress the same car that had been following them turned into the parking lot and pulled in two stalls over from where they sat with the engine idling. She watched in disbelief as two men who looked Chinese got out and walked toward them. *Were those the men from the parking lot at the jail?* Her disbelief turned to panic when she saw they were carrying guns.

"When I tell you, you're going to hit the gas."

Constance seemed to be busying herself pulling something from the pocket of her jean jacket. Suzanne wanted to ask her what self-respecting woman wears a jean jacket, especially in the twenty-first century, but she was more concerned with her instructions to hit the gas, because it meant they would be going up over the curb.

"Won't that damage my oil pan? Or my tires? And what about the front end alignment? These Cadillacs aren't cheap to repair, you know."

But Constance Void didn't answer. The Chinamen were approaching rapidly and everything was happening so fast Suzanne quickly forgot to worry about her precious Cadillac or the fashion statement Constance was making with that jean jacket.

It seemed to her Constance Void had seemingly developed the arms of Shiva as she pressed the button to lower the front passenger window with one hand while holding the thing she'd taken from her pocket below the dashboard with the other hand and flicking her lighter with yet another hand. It was dizzying. For a moment Suzanne thought Constance was lighting up some of her devil weed in her car and all she could think about was the smoke ruining the Laura Ashley upholstery. But then it started to spark. Constance Void had lit the fuse to a firecracker.

If they searched her at the jail they most definitely found the firecracker.

Her mind was racing in pointless directions, considering the situation. *So why did they give it back to her? Why would the Oxnard Police let her keep a firecracker? Is this another one of those Hispanics and fireworks kind of things?* Suzanne was certain she would never understand that whole Hispanics and fireworks thing.

What happened next was something the likes of which Suzanne had only ever seen in movies, the kind her husband liked to watch after she'd gone to bed. Smiling pleasantly at the approaching Chinamen, Constance said something that Suzanne assumed was in Mandarin or one of those other nonsensical languages they've got in China, and then tossed the firecracker to the ground at their feet. At the same time, a bell began to ring. Suzanne had programmed the notifications on her iPhone to ring every night at the same time to remind her to take her Ambien so she would be sound asleep when her husband came to bed. For obvious reasons she didn't care to discuss.

"Punch it!"

Constance lunged and grabbed the steering wheel. Suzanne did as Constance instructed, largely because the Chinamen had aimed their guns right at them and she couldn't think of any other option. Constance cranked the wheel as Suzanne mashed the gas pedal with her foot and crouched as low as she could. Even though she couldn't see out the front, from her crouched position she watched the underside of the palm tree in front of the Krispy Kreme fly past and then the awning over the drive-up window as they passed through the motorist lane and came out on the other side of the building.

Suzanne heard more than one loud pop and was pretty sure they weren't all just firecrackers because Constance had only tossed the one that she knew of. Plus, she was almost certain her back window had shattered and something whizzed past her head. Reflexively, she reached up and felt her hair for shrapnel, or whatever it is that's supposed to fly around when people are shooting guns at perfectly nice therapists and their delusional clients.

Constance was shouting at her to slide over as she kept her hands on the wheel and for a few awkward moments was sitting on top of Suzanne as she continued to keep the gas pedal to the floor and they flew out of the parking lot back onto Rose Avenue.

"I've got it, bitch! Get yourself out from under me and for gawd's sake take your foot off the gas pedal! The freeway entrance is coming up and I can't make the turn at this speed!"

Suzanne could see she was absolutely right about her client because Constance Void was still clearly exhibiting symptoms of being delusional. The licensed marriage and family therapist knew she was not a bitch, and would tell you to just ask her husband, but he hadn't been coming home much lately.

But she did comply with her demand, largely because she had proven to know what she was talking about back there with the Chinamen and their guns. And she had to admit, Constance Void's firecracker defense is something that should be taught in those high school self-defense classes for girls.

Suzanne was pretty sure they were still making them take that class their senior year at Oxnard High, where they give all the girls cans of pepper spray at graduation to carry on their key chain. Until this incident with the Chinamen, Suzanne had always considered that whole thing to be a waste of funding, because the most sensible thing was obviously to teach girls to stop trying to take back the night, and for heaven's sake stop being out in public alone. It's just not proper. And don't ever get Suzanne Shill started on the way those girls dress. You really don't want to go there.

Watching behind them as Constance barreled down the Ventura freeway, Suzanne wasn't seeing the Chinamen's car. She wasn't entirely sure why, but It didn't surprise her one bit that Constance Void could drive like she was possessed.

Before Suzanne knew what was happening, Constance had them off the freeway and winding through the back roads of Ventura County toward Simi. Demanding to know where they were going and why she didn't just drive straight back to the Oxnard Police

Department, Suzanne felt she was doing a masterful job of regaining control of the situation from her client. Unfortunately, Constance just shook her head and frowned.

"Are you kidding?"

She was laughing and Suzanne couldn't for the life of her see why. "You honestly think the Oxnard Police are a match for the Chinamen?" Considering she'd just seen Constance defeat two armed men with nothing more than a firecracker, to Suzanne the logical answer was *yes*.

"We got lucky with that one. Those guys are operatives of the most ruthless organized crime syndicate on the planet. And I've just pissed them off."

Constance explained that it all started when she decided to try her hand at a new potion to make teenage Hispanic boys stop hitting on her when she was out for her evening power walks. She'd made the mistake of telling them she was old enough to be their grandmother, which she thought would turn them off, but only made the situation worse, since every Hispanic boy dreams of being with an *abuela* for his first sexual conquest.

"Do I really need to explain to you that the word *abuela* is Spanish for *grandmother;* or have you spent enough time in Oxnard to know that one?"

Constance Void was the victim of her own cultural ignorance, and if she'd known the trouble it was going to get her into, would have kept her mouth shut and just ignored their salacious taunting.

"I'd sent out some smoke signals for advice on what to put in the potion, and got several good replies. One in particular sounded the most promising, but it involved an ingredient I knew I'd need to acquire from some sketchy people."

Suzanne had to wonder if by *sketchy* she meant the gun carrying Chinamen whom they had just outrun. If so, the term *sketchy* seemed woefully inadequate.

Constance went on to say she made a trip down to L.A. and met with a lovely Chinese herbalist who told her for a fee he would acquire the mysterious powdered substance she needed and send someone up to Oxnard to deliver it to her. Unfortunately, it wasn't until she had it in her hand that she truly understood what she had just purchased, and from whom.

Thinking she was getting a rare strain of powdered ginseng, Constance Void was told by the courier she had actually purchased powdered human testes, the essential ingredient necessary in making a potion to stop testosterone-fueled teenage Hispanics in their tracks. And in so doing, she had gotten herself mixed up with the worst element of the Chinese black market:

human organ traffickers.

When their courier was picked up by the Oxnard Police along with Constance, she was certain it set off alarms in their organization, especially when she was released but he was not. As she and Suzanne left the police department she recognized the car the courier's companions had been driving earlier, and watched as they followed the women out into traffic.

Suzanne sat in stunned silence as Constance explained and they wound their way through the dark unlit back roads of Ventura County toward Simi.

"The only thing we can do at this point is put as much distance as possible between ourselves and the Chinamen. Which means either leaving California altogether or finding someplace safe to hide out until things blow over."

Suzanne wasn't about to go on the road with anyone who was so delusional they thought they could solve their problems with pot and voodoo potions, especially considering the many railway crossings she might be finding herself crossing with a client deeply obsessed with train wrecks. Nor could she begin to imagine where the two of them could safely hide out together. She was having trouble just being in the same car with the Void. If only she had listened to her instincts and insisted her client consider hospitalization at their very first session, all of this could have been avoided.

And then it hit her. Back in Camarillo was that treatment facility where she had admitting privileges. She reached for her iPhone and told Constance to turn around.

"You're going to need to go along with me on this and tell them you're hearing voices."

"Tell who what? I never told you about the voices." Seeing Suzanne searching through her phone's address book, the Void lowered the window before grabbing the iPhone from the therapist's hand and tossing it out the window into the night.

"What did you do that for!?" Suzanne wasn't exactly screaming, and she wasn't exactly shouting. She had skipped both and gone directly to screeching.

"They may not have been able to follow us, but those Chinese are the best electronic trackers on the planet. I guarantee you they already have your full name, address, and cell phone number. Not only are they waiting for you to place a call, they can triangulate our location with it."

Suzanne considered calling the facility from a pay phone, but there are no pay phones in Camarillo. If Adam Levine had escaped from under his desk during a robbery of his bank in Camarillo, Maroon 5 would never have written the pop ballad Payphone. Had Constance Void been around he might have flagged her down and asked to use her cell, but everyone knows the Void only uses smoke signals. Music video director Samuel Bayer would have ended up filming the action in the bottom of a bong and Billboard Hot 100 charts would have been changed forever.

In the absence of both phone and the necessary tools for smoke signals, Suzanne decided walking into the facility unannounced with her client might actually work better since it elevated the drama factor and gave the situation more of a sense of urgency. If there was anything Suzanne Shill loved, it was the drama that came from an elevated sense of urgency.

She gave directions to Constance and both women agreed it would be safest to park the Cadillac in front of the Ralph's Grocery half a mile from the facility, since it was also only a matter of time before the Chinese hacked into the car's GPS and located it. Leaving it as far from the treatment facility as possible was the safest course of action.

Suzanne Shill took one last look over her shoulder at her bullet riddled car with the broken out back window as the two women walked away. Half a block later she slipped out of her pumps and slung them over her shoulder. Another half a block later she announced that she was pretty sure she'd just picked up tuberculosis, staph, and Ebola from walking barefoot on the sidewalk. But Constance knew better.

"No, this is Camarillo. Camarillo is a bedroom community. The only diseases in a bedroom community are sexually transmitted."

They walked in silence for another block before something else occurred to the therapist.

"But what about my clients? What are they going to do without me?"

In an uncharacteristic display of self-restraint, Constance Void didn't say what she was thinking, which was the therapist's clients would be better off without her.

She had surmised that very thing on her first and only visit to Suzanne Shill's office, when the court-appointed therapist arrived several minutes late and apologized for the delay by explaining she had three clients in the hospital she'd needed to visit. Constance thought it was entirely possible that those were the only three clients the therapist had other than her.

Unless of course you counted that poor defendant she'd been unable to testify for, who was probably going to prison. And it hadn't escaped the Void's attention that prisons seemed to be housing a lot of mental patients these days, so really what difference was there anymore between that and a mental hospital?

As the two women walked in the dim street light of the Camarillo night, Suzanne replayed the events of the evening and remembered Constance saying something to the Chinamen just before the gunfire erupted. *But what had she said?*

"Please ring the bell because the house has three floors and the pudding is at the top." To Constance it was perfectly obvious and she was somewhat annoyed at being asked.

"I try to learn a necessary phrase in every language just in case I find myself someplace unexpected where I need to ask for directions."

Suzanne considered asking her just how that phrase would be necessary if she ever needed to find her way around Beijing, but decided against it. The wine had left her with a headache, her feet hurt, and she was inexplicably craving pudding. More than anything, she found herself hoping the rehab center served pudding in a cup in the cafeteria. Chocolate pudding in a cup.

She still had no idea what she was going to do with herself once she had Constance safely admitted, but the therapist considered it unprofessional to burden her client with her uncertainty. If ever there was a moment for comfort food, this was it. As they approached the entrance to the Pleasant Valley Sunday Rehabilitation and Psychiatric Treatment Center, Constance let out a low whistle.

"Welcome to the Hotel California. Such a lovely place. Is it one of those places where you can check out but you can never leave?"

Suzanne Shill couldn't be entirely sure because she'd spoken under her breath, but she thought maybe Constance Void was finally starting to get a grip on reality.

CHAPTER THREE

The only thing Agent Toole liked more than monitor cloning was activating a target's cell phone microphone remotely and listening in on their conversations.

Few cell phone owners truly understand that because of the battery, the microphone is always on – even when the phone is turned off. And it made his job so much easier. He was able to listen in on that first therapy session and learn, in real time, that Suzanne Shill was agreeing to do online therapy with Constance Void because of some kind of objection the client had with the throw pillows in her waiting room and also an apparent train wreck that Toole was unable to get any intel on.

But online therapy was ideal for the NSA agent because it allowed him to not just follow along, but print transcripts of every exchange between the therapist and her client. And because the Patriot Act abolished doctor-client privilege in matters of national security, Toole was well within his rights as an agent of the NSA to print, copy, store, analyze and discuss the exchanges between the therapist and her client with complete impunity.

Once he'd returned to the office and reported his findings in Ventura to his supervisor, things started moving pretty quickly around Agent Toole's cubicle. His clearance code was upgraded, which meant a lot of the investigation was up to his own discretion, and his other assignments were either delegated or put on a back burner.

Toole liked his newfound freedom. He could already taste the sunlight filtering through the smog and in through the window of that new office he knew the investigation would be earning him. Maybe if things went really well, he could transfer to a nice corner office in one of those new buildings in Utah.

He was especially relieved he'd been listening in when Suzanne Shill got the call from the Void about being picked up by the Oxnard Police, because it allowed him to closely follow the confrontation the women had with the Chinese. He wasn't surprised the Chinese were involved – no operation of this magnitude could possibly be off the radar of the Chinese.

While he knew it was possible the shootout at the Krispy Kreme could have been just for show, especially when he saw the Void's firecracker defense on the security camera footage, he doubted it. Instinct led the agent to suspect it meant Constance Void was most likely not actually working with the Chinese, which would have been the obvious assumption. Toole was too smart for that. He was well aware while China and Israel were economic bed partners there are always issues that rear their ugly heads between bed partners once the honeymoon is over. He was certain his heightened dot-connecting skills were going to come in handy with this investigation.

When the feed from Suzanne's cell phone went dead he had a pretty good idea what happened to it, which also confirmed what he'd been suspecting about Constance Void's level of professional training. She was without question expert in taking evasive action. In anticipation of her making the therapist discard her cell phone, he had already accessed the Cadillac's GPS and OnStar system, which allowed him to both listen in on them and track their location. He also blocked the OnStar feed and jammed the GPS transmission to prevent the Chinese from either tracking them or getting any intel on their destination.

Watching the feed from the Camarillo Ralph's security camera, he saw the two women leave the car in the parking lot and head south on foot toward the industrial section of the suburb. Each step of the way, Agent Toole was observing and then deleting the feed from surveillance cameras outside businesses they passed.

He suspected they were going to the perfect place for them, especially with his help obscuring any electronic footprint they might inadvertently leave. He could only assume the Chinese hadn't gotten the jump on him, since they would have done exactly the same thing he was doing. The last view he got of them was when they paused in front of Hung Lo's Chinese restaurant and the therapist removed her shoes. After that they walked out of range of the security camera.

Toole lingered briefly over the thought the women stopping in front of a Chinese restaurant was significant, but after what he had witnessed at the Krispy Kreme he considered it a remote possibility.

Once he analyzed the footage carefully, he concluded neither woman appeared to be leaving anything behind that could be concealing a coded message. Nor did he see any smoke signals.

Although there were no records in any database to support his theory, Toole was certain the women were headed to a nearby rehabilitation center and psychiatric treatment facility where Suzanne Shill most likely had admitting privileges. He admired the resourcefulness of the two women. They would be untraceable as long as they kept their heads and admitted Constance under an assumed name. With her level of training and experience, he was certain they would do just that.

It was also the perfect place to have the Void under surveillance, since every employee at the center had a cell phone in their pocket, and there were surveillance cameras in almost every room. Those rooms that didn't have them had clinic computers and staff laptops with built in web cameras. With any luck, Toole would be able to observe her sending her infamous smoke signals, and get a better sense of how she keeps managing to locate so many train wrecks. Hadn't there been a terror attack at a train station in China not long ago, one with a bomb? He made a note to dig into the ties between Chinese and Israeli intelligence, looking for the presence of both at recent terror attacks involving trains.

Agent Toole was fairly certain that in short order he would be reporting to his supervisor the identities of the Mossad agents that had formed a questionable alliance with the Chinese and were being aided by a traitor from our own government in Ventura County.

Something kept telling him it was no accident that this investigation was centered in that county. Not only did it have two strategically located military bases on its coast, but both of them are nuclear, which meant time was unquestionably of the essence.

The agent had found himself thinking about Ventura more and more since returning to his cubicle, and for some reason he had begun craving pudding in a cup. Chocolate pudding in a cup. Leaning back in his computer chair and propping his feet up on his desk, he gave a satisfied sigh as he pulled the little foil top off his third one in a row and lingered over the thought of a pretty bailiff's hazel eyes as he licked chocolate pudding off a plastic spoon.

And then it hit him. As often is the case when relaxing into a nice satisfying cup of pudding knocks loose those things that need knocking loose, it came to him he had overlooked something important: robes. More specifically, men in robes. That was the key. It had to be. What else could it mean that the Void had mentioned men in robes to him in the courtroom and also mentioned them in her coded message? He was certain it was unintentional, and that slip-up had given him just the advantage he needed.

He also didn't think it was any coincidence many Israeli men wear robes. It was the last dot Mossad would ever expect the NSA to connect.

CHAPTER FOUR

Camarillo's Pleasant Valley Sunday Rehabilitation and
Psychiatric Treatment Center sits atop a gentle slope in
that curious junction one often finds between a
bedroom community's residential and industrial
districts. The hacienda style pink stucco building
houses both substance abusers undergoing
rehabilitation and psychiatric patients seeking respite
from whatever mental and emotional demons may be
possessing them at the time. While some may think
shoving alcoholics and schizophrenics together in the
same treatment center is questionable, the economics
of our time have a differing opinion.

At first Suzanne Shill thought the reason she woke
to the taste of dirty mop in her mouth was because
she'd been dreaming she was dancing with one of the
animated mops from the Disney movie, Fantasia. Only,
among the dancing mops were leaf blowers that
seemed to be ejaculating chocolate pudding all over

the walls of the broom closet. But as she lay there in the faint light that seeped through the crack beneath the door she realized the taste in her mouth was from the rag mop she'd used as a pillow.

After seeing to it her client got settled into her room for the night Suzanne had slipped down a back stairway to the basement and found a utility closet where she managed to get relatively comfortable among the cleaning supplies. Hoping there would be no urgent need for mops or push brooms or scouring powder during the night, the therapist curled up on a pile of cleaning rags and fell asleep as soon as her head hit the mop. Without Ambien.

But now as she glanced at her watch and saw she still had at least an hour before she could make a convincing entrance under the guise of visiting her client, all the thoughts which would otherwise have kept her awake flooded her mind. First and foremost was the issue of her husband. He would have noticed her absence by now, perhaps even begun placing some calls. If Constance Void was right and the Chinese were watching both her home and phone, how was she going to get word to her husband that she was all right?

Second, there was the issue of the Chinese organ traffickers. How long was she going to have to hide from them? Suzanne had never run from anyone or anything in her life, unless you counted the Ambien she took at bedtime. More than anything, she resented that the first time she did it was from foreigners she was running. What's worse, it was from atheist foreigners.

It didn't surprise her atheists would be trafficking in illegal human organs. Atheists have no morals. A Christian would never do anything like that, nor would he ever launch an unprovoked attack on innocent, unsuspecting people. And without question, one would never shoot at another Christian in a Krispy Kreme parking lot. Of that Suzanne was certain.

Opening the door a crack to let in enough light, Suzanne reached for the hook where she'd hung her dress and pulled it back on over the slip she had no choice but to sleep in. Leaving the shoes off, she tiptoed to the lavatory directly across from the broom closet and splashed her face with cold water. Although the mirror above the dirty porcelain sink was cracked, it didn't keep her from getting a good look at the disaster that was her hair. Even the little sample sized hair products and travel styling brush from her purse wouldn't be enough to salvage what had been her signature hairdo her entire adult life.

With a heavy sigh, Suzanne resigned herself to wearing her chestnut brown hair down around her face, the neatly trimmed ends just brushing her shoulders. At least she had her travel makeup kit. After removing the remnants of yesterday's eye makeup, she reapplied a fresh coat and told herself it would have to do. She may not know how long she would be in hiding, or how she was going to get word to her husband, and she may not have the power derived from her signature hairdo, but at least she had a fresh coat of lady paint. Small consolation, but sometimes a woman's just got to make do.

When she spotted the white lab coat hanging on the back of the lavatory door, she thought it might be the perfect way to cover up the shame of wearing the same dress she'd had on the day before, as well as hide the curious stains she found on it. They looked to her like chocolate pudding, but for the life of her Suzanne could not remember having eaten any pudding the previous day. She dismissed the notion it had anything to do with the dream she'd had. Pudding is, after all, just pudding.

Slipping the lab coat on over her dress, she buttoned it up and reached into the pocket as she checked herself in the broken mirror. Discovering a thick silver hair clip and a pair of black framed reading glasses, Suzanne pulled her hair back, and clipping it into a wide pony tail, put on the glasses. Looking back at her through the cracked mirror was a powerful, competent, resourceful woman, but all she could see was a very hungry woman who could not stop thinking about pudding.

Carrying her pumps as she tiptoed up the stairs and peered through the door before slipping them on and entering the deserted hallway, the aroma of breakfast foods hit her olfactory senses the way a drunken shopping cart hits the curb: with a bang and spinning wheels. And much like that drunken shopping cart's wheels, her appetite was spinning shamelessly. She deeply regretted having only had wine and water crackers for dinner.

As much as she wanted those spinning wheels to take her where her hunger begged her to, she needed to find Constance first. Walking into the cafeteria without her client by her side might very well raise suspicions about her being at the rehab center at such an early hour. The last thing Suzanne Shill needed was to raise suspicions this early in the game of hiding from Chinese illegal organ traffickers.

At this point, we can only hope the drunken shopping cart gets itself into rehab before it wakes up to discover it has no wheels because someone's harvested them. Possibly an atheist Chinaman. Or Mossad.

For the first time in her career, Suzanne found the click-click-clicking of her pumps somewhat disconcerting as she walked down the hall toward the wing her client had been assigned to. For one thing, it was too loud for this early in the morning, and for another thing it sent the wrong message. It was a message about fashion correctness that was entirely incorrect in both the setting and the disguise she had put together. She had just begun to consider how she could best go about correcting the incorrect footwear situation when something moving in the courtyard on the other side of the hallway's outer windows caught her attention.

Through the mist rising from the sparse drought resistant landscaping and patio tables adorning the courtyard at the center of the facility, Suzanne could see Constance Void moving in slow motion to some unseen inspiration. *Is she dancing to music in slow motion? Why?* As she stood there puzzling over what her client was doing, a voice startled her. In hospital issued robe and pajamas the patient had shuffled up to her noiselessly in his blue fuzzy hospital issued slipper socks and stood next to her.

"T'ai Chi. Terrifying. Absolutely terrifying." Suzanne wasn't sure she'd ever seen such an easily frightened Hispanic. She always thought of them as fearless. Why else would they come here and expose themselves to all those toxic agricultural chemicals?

He shuddered so violently he wrapped his arms around himself as though it would keep him from crumbling, and turned away. Before she could ask him what he found terrifying about it he scurried off, repeatedly looking over his shoulder nervously, seemingly afraid the woman doing T'ai Chi in the courtyard might lunge through the window and come after him. And Suzanne didn't know why.

She'd heard of T'ai Chi. She knew that it, like yoga and meditation, was a tool of the devil. But as she stood there watching the silent slow motion dance, she couldn't for the life of her figure out what made it so threatening. To anyone.

"Zann?"

Startled by a voice behind her, Suzanne turned around with about as much grace as a drunken shopping cart.

"Are you Zann Killjoy?"

When Suzanne was admitting Constance the night before, they didn't think it was enough to just give Constance an assumed identity. The Chinese would be looking for two women, and since medical records are all electronic now, it would be what anyone hacking into the electronic medical records system would be

looking for. So she told the admitting nurse she was
going through a divorce and in the process of
reclaiming her maiden name, and would like it if they
would put that in her patient's records instead of *Shill*.
She also told the nurse she preferred to be called Zann,
thinking by shortening her name it would sound
ambiguously male.

She was stuck with Killjoy because when the
nurse asked Suzanne who she was, before she could
answer Constance butted in and said, "Oh that's the
killjoy." So she was stuck with the name.

"You must be our new patient's therapist." The
man was smiling warmly as he extended his hand.
"How is Morgan La Fay today?"

Suzanne was having a hard time adjusting to the
new names both women had adopted. But as the
uncommonly handsome African-American continued
to smile warmly and she returned his handshake, she
felt a strange stirring beneath the buttons of her lab
coat when he said the name Zann. This was something
she could learn to live with.

Dr. Ben Carlson was Pleasant Valley Sunday's
only full-time resident psychiatrist. He was, in fact, a
psychiatric neurosurgeon of some renown. Suzanne
was speechless, having read one of his published
papers in graduate school and been deeply impressed

with his insights. He warmly welcomed her to the center and invited her into his office for a briefing about her client before breakfast.

Although he stood a full head taller than her, their matching lab coats gave Suzanne a sense they were equals in a way she had never felt with any psychiatrist she had worked with. For that matter, she had never felt it with any man, and scolded herself for even briefly entertaining the notion women could ever be their equals. That just wasn't God's plan.

The doctor nodded for her to take the chair across from his desk. "Your client has already caused quite a stir. And while I try to stay open-minded about what she's doing out there in the courtyard, the truth is T'ai Chi is a martial art. I just don't think most of our patients can handle being exposed to that. It's simply too threatening. This is a pretty vulnerable population we've got here, as I'm sure you are well aware."

"Is that why that one patient was so terrified of her?" Suzanne relaxed into the overstuffed pleather chair with a curious mix of confidence and nervousness. Something about the combination of the doctor's gentle soothing voice along with those dark eyes and impossibly long lashes was triggering something in her that she wasn't sure she was comfortable with. She was, after all, a married woman.

"Carlos? He's our resident pantheist. Everything terrifies him."

"Why would a pantheist be terrified of everything? Don't they believe that everything in existence is part of an all-encompassing god, making all things one?" Dr. Carlson nodded his head and smiled curiously.

"So what is he afraid of?"

"He's a xenophobic pantheist. Yes, he believes that everything is interconnected and equally the same. But he also watches a lot of Flocks News, which has become central command for xenophobia in America. So he's gripped by a belief that anything different from him is a threat. He's terrified of everything. Including himself. Especially himself because he's so different, since his beliefs take such a radical departure from what other pantheists believe. Basically, he's too different to live comfortably in his own skin. Before being crippled by these afflictions he was a respected anthropologist."

Suzanne had noticed the television was tuned to Flocks News when she passed the day room on her way to the Void's room with her client the night before. Flocks News was the tragically popular division of Twentieth Century Flocks. The network catered exclusively to people who need to be told who to follow, who to hate and what to think.

"You don't seem to be bothered by the effects of Flocks News on him, or on any of the patients, considering I saw a sign above the television in the day room forbidding anyone from changing the channel. Why?"

One could argue he was taking a calculated risk by being honest with Suzanne. But unless one actually knew Dr. Carlson and was familiar with his overwhelming sense of superiority over others, especially over women and the mentally ill, one wouldn't know he was always bluntly honest in his delivery of his version of the truth, which was shaped largely by the evangelical fundamentalists he was exposed to in his formative years.

"I don't approve of either pantheism or anthropology. Hippie nonsense, if you ask me. The more he's exposed to Flocks News, the more he will forget those beliefs from his former life and fall into lock-step with a healthier point of view, one that will keep him at a distance from others. Nobody needs those notions anthropologists like him bring out of the jungles with them. It's best for all concerned he forgets those heathen tribal chants and incantations. They're straight out of Satan's playbook, every one of them. Hopefully, our missionaries have gone into those jungles and made sure nobody remembers them. Memory can be a troublesome thing, don't you agree?"

Suzanne nodded absently and decided against asking what led Carlos to being hospitalized in the first place. She knew better than anyone there doesn't really need to be much reason. And forcing herself to not think about it was making her uncomfortable.

The doctor reached for his prescription pad and effortlessly steered the conversation away from the xenophobic pantheist. "Speaking of being uncomfortable in one's own skin, I understand your client is hearing voices. How is she managing with that? You didn't list what medications she's on." Suzanne's mind raced to remember the details of the cover story she'd used in admitting her client.

Yes to voices, no to medication because. Because. Because what?

"I don't see that they're interfering greatly with her quality of life." She was improvising and it surprised her. It was the kind of thing she would never ordinarily say, since anyone who didn't live the way she did had an entirely unacceptable quality of life. "She seems to have taken it all in stride, adopting a kind of philosophy about the voices."

"So you don't get the sense they're telling her to hurt herself or others?"

"No, not at all."

"So why are you admitting her?"

"Because I'm concerned she may be slipping into a psychosis made up of overlapping delusions. Possibly pot induced."

She explained the client's delusion about being a *court steganographer,* and shared something Constance had told her during their first session. "She also believes she is a prescient dreamer, claiming things she dreams come true. She says she sees certain events in her dreams and it helps her to be better prepared for them when the events unfold in her waking life."

"Like what?" The doctor leaned forward in his chair, suddenly intrigued.

"Like dreaming she saw a woman who was a blind native American midget being helped at a crosswalk by a native American boy in a Mohawk wearing a Boy Scout uniform. And then seeing exactly that the very next morning while sitting in traffic."

"And you don't believe her?"

"It's not that I don't believe her. It's that I don't see the point. In what way did she need to be prepared to see that? Nothing happened. When I asked her, she said that the universe is helping her to celebrate the random by giving her a heads up about random events.

It just doesn't add up. The universe itself is just....the universe. It's not omniscient. And the random isn't an entity. It's just random.

Also, she refuses to use the politically correct term *little people*. When I confronted her about how inappropriate it is to call them midgets, she simply said the midgets let her call them that. If that's not delusional, I don't know what is."

She went on to explain her client also considered herself some sort of empath. She didn't just feel things others felt, she smelled what others were smelling too. It made being in some cities almost unbearable.

"Why would the ability to smell what others are smelling do that?"

"She mentioned San Francisco as an example. She says it reeks of urine so badly even when she goes indoors she continues to smell it through the olfactory senses of other people out on the street. So she never goes there."

"What about these feelings you say she gets from others?"

"She said it's especially strong when she's near someone who's ill or injured. She not only feels it, but knows exactly what it is. The example she gave was the time she was in a book store in downtown Ventura and a woman was offering Kirilian photographs of people for five dollars. Morgan looked down at the sample photographs she had on display and pointed to one, demanding to know the whereabouts of the person in the picture. The woman said it was her husband who was in the booth manning the camera. Morgan told the woman to get him to a hospital immediately."

Ben Carlson was certain Suzanne was going to say the woman ignored her advice, as any sane person would do. But she didn't. She said the woman grabbed her arm and asked Morgan if it was his liver. When she said yes the woman started to cry, saying she had been suspecting his cancer had relapsed.

"She went on to say she was sick for four days with liver cancer until she was able to shake it off. Actually, that's the other reason she says she goes to the courtroom. She says she's trying to desensitize herself to the feelings of others, since she feels emotional pain in others as strongly as she feels physical pain. In fact, she insists there really isn't any difference between the two.

Here's my whole take on her claim she's having prescient dreams: if the gift of prophecy isn't clearly leading the dreamer to the work of the Lord, it's obviously of the devil. And as far as this empathic nonsense goes, I think it's a construct of her delusional system, doctor. Plain and simple. Most likely induced by both pot and influences outside her control, like demons."

Dr. Carlson smiled and leaned back in his chair. He had a feeling he and Zann were going to get along very well. While he wouldn't know for sure whether her client was indeed being used by Satan until meeting with Morgan La Fay, he was happy Suzanne was open to the idea such things could happen. He was confident he would have no trouble determining how serious the demonic possession of Zann's client was and the right course of action to take.

As it turns out, Dr. Benjamin Carlson was certain God had been behind the prescient dream he'd had in medical school which enabled him to become the psychiatric neurosurgeon he is today. As a sophomore in pre-med, the young Ben Carlson neglected to study for his chemistry final. In fact, he pretty much slacked off in the class all semester. The night before the exam he dreamed each and every one of the equations that were in the test. Including the answers. Not only did he pass the test because of it, he didn't get a single answer wrong, so it brought up his average for the semester and got him on the honor roll. Ben Carlson had told the story many times, and each time he attributed it to God.

This time, as he told the story to Suzanne, the

goosebumps it gave her were overshadowed only by the warmth swelling in her chest as it threatened to pop the buttons of her lab coat. It was making her question her beliefs for the first time, specifically the one about marriage being for life. Submitting to her husband in headship sounded good on paper, but in practice she was finding it took a lot of Ambien to keep pretending to be enthusiastic about it.

"So you think there might be a chance her prescient dreams and empathic disorder are real, and not the product of a delusional system?"

The doctor nodded confidently and leaned back in his chair.

"The important thing here is to be able to discern whether it is in fact the devil himself who is behind it, or merely one of his lesser demons. I look forward to working with her and finding out. Perhaps her delusion about being a *court steganographer* is a clue we need to look at more closely. Plus, this close personal relationship she claims she has with both the random and these midgets warrants investigating. And I don't think you need to worry about her getting into any pot here, so if there have been any symptoms of a pot induced psychosis, they should dissipate soon.

If not, it may be an indicator that Satan really is behind her pathology, in which case I have developed a simple surgical technique that will prevent the dreams and other notions from infiltrating her thoughts. The less the devil is able to infiltrate one's thoughts, the less likely it is one will become possessed by the dark lord's demons."

There was one other possibility regarding the client's empathic issues, but the doctor needed to do some research before saying anything about it. If it was what he was suspecting, his surgery was definitely the only option. Neuroscience may think it had all the answers, but Ben Carlson was pretty sure it was getting those answers from the devil.

Thinking it might give her a good reason for being seen at the rehab center so much, Suzanne suggested she spend as much time as possible there for a while, both to observe her client and to keep her from engaging in any martial arts that might seem menacing to the other patients. Doctor Carlson agreed, and offered her the use of one of the unoccupied offices during her visits.

"I find it easier to maintain doctor-patient boundaries when I'm working with patients in the more formal setting of an office. Some doctors are happy to do their sessions anywhere with their patients, even out in the courtyard, but I'm not one of them."

As he ushered her out into the hallway and

unlocked the door to the office just three doors down from his own, Ben Carlson slid the key into her hand. For a brief moment his finger lingered in the center of her palm and their eyes met. Her mouth went dry as Suzanne realized they were having a moment. She also realized she had a place to sleep, since the office he was giving her had a sofa in it. And it had throw pillows. They weren't Laura Ashley, but they would do better than a rag mop.

The two trained professionals stood staring into each other's eyes until the moment was interrupted by the sound of Constance Void clearing her throat.

"Hey, Killjoy. Breakfast time. I can't wait to tell you about the dream I had last night. Two other people here had the exact same dream. About pudding. And leaf blowers. My favorite. Don't you just love it?"

Suzanne's eyes met Dr. Carlson's and a thin smile of recognition flickered across his face. She was relieved to finally have someone who understood what she was up against.

The Void just grinned.

"It's like I always say, celebrate the random, dude."

CHAPTER FIVE

Men in robes. The search was on, and Agent Toole
knew he was up to the task. He had done an exhaustive
search of the database for all known organizations in
America where men are known for routinely wearing
robes. It surprised him to learn it was so common.
Aside from the obvious Israeli connection, there was
the possibility the Rastafarians were involved. And of
course, he couldn't dismiss the Catholics, considering
how much those men love their robes. And then there
were the Buddhists, and of course the Muslims. And
what about men's acapella groups and non-
denominational church choirs? And the Klansmen?
The list was getting longer. Toole realized his
investigation could take much more time than he'd first
anticipated.

   He quickly dismissed the Buddhists, and there
really was no point looking into the Muslims. Who
wasn't looking into the Muslims? As for the Klansmen,

they were doing exactly what was expected of them. The intelligence community was well aware the lower the intelligence of an organization's members, the easier it is to both manipulate and predict their behavior.

He looked briefly at the Buddhists and saw only that the Dharma Center in Los Angeles was hosting some visiting Shaolin Monks, where they would be making some kind of mandala. Toole was pretty sure a bunch of Buddhist monks playing with sand was nothing anyone needed to be worried about. As for the Muslims, he was confident the close scrutiny they were already getting due to the color of their skin and the colorfully scripted fear alerts released periodically left him with nothing to discover about them which wasn't already known.

And while the first most obvious place for him to start the investigation was the Los Angeles Catholic Archdiocese, he decided to first cover the Rastafarian angle because of how many times the Void had mentioned them in the coded message he'd intercepted.

Expecting to find the usual electronic footprint, including email addresses, cell phones and banking records, Toole was surprised to find the Rastafarians had none. Not the slightest hint of an electronic trail of bread crumbs. Or would that be cookie crumbs? Oh sure, they had a website for the First Church of Rasta in Los Angeles, with a phone number and email address listed on it. But none of it was actually connected in any way to a traceable person or organization. All attempts to trace the accounts used to open the website led him to dead ends. Toole knew it was significant these people had gone to such lengths to cover their tracks.

Why are these people so elusive? What have they got to hide? He pondered the curiously conspicuous dead end as he sat in his cubicle absently licking his plastic spoon. *And how is the NSA supposed to collect and study their metadata if they don't have any?*

Considering the power the Rastafarians must have to be able to manage the most dangerous Mossad agents on the planet, the more he thought about it the more it made sense he wouldn't be able to simply set up an electronic surveillance and find out what he needed to. This case was going to require human *intel*. It was what he was born for. Toole decided he would start by going on a stakeout to the First Church of Rasta in the City of Venice. He knew it was risky, but it had to be done. The clock was ticking.

The first obstacle he had to overcome on the stakeout was the impossibility of finding parking on West Venice Boulevard. How was anyone supposed to stake out a business when they couldn't find parking anywhere near it? He knew he could have driven one of the fleet cars with its government plates and flashed his credentials to anyone who might challenge his right to park wherever he wanted. But something told Toole that sitting in a gray Sebring sedan with government plates outside any business was a surefire way to say, "I'm watching you."

So the intrepid stellar field agent-to-be did the best he could: he parked his car in one of the overpriced all-day lots several blocks away and did his surveillance standing across the street from the Church of Rasta.

Of course, the second obstacle he had to overcome was the discomfort of the disguise he'd worn. Because the NSA doesn't make a practice of sending the field agents it doesn't have on surveillance in disguise, Toole took it upon himself to go to a costume shop in Culver City to find something suitable, and was impressed with what he'd managed to put together.

Because he knew all Rastafarians are basically just hippies in robes with confusing hair who smoke a lot of pot, he found a fringed suede jacket and bell bottom jeans he was certain would allow him to blend in with the Venice crowd. It was the kind of disguise a poorly trained undercover narcotics officer in Eastern

Oregon would wear. Especially if his objective is to terrorize a middle aged medical marijuana patient with the hopes she might slip up and admit she's the hardened criminal he needs her to be so he can meet his arrest quota for the month. But that's not what crossed his mind when Toole looked at himself in the mirror. What crossed his mind was how easy the whole business of being a field agent was turning out to be.

While the costume itself was rather comfortable, he had to invest in a long frizzy wig and sunglasses with round frames in order to complete the look. And as any poorly trained undercover narcotics officer in Eastern Oregon would have told him, those wigs get hot. And once they get hot, they itch. So it wasn't long before he found himself standing in the Southern California heat with the full sun bouncing off the sidewalk, at which point it crawled up the leg of his bell bottoms and lit the wig on fire. And then it began to itch.

Toole tried to look casual as he stood in the scorching heat pretending he wasn't really wearing a bad wig that itched because it was on fire. He would have asked himself why he didn't just dress as a tourist, since that was really all he saw passing by as he stood there. But the wig had become a smoldering wad of buttered steel wool sliding across his head each time he reached up and scratched it.

Keeping track of its position on his head had become his primary objective. One minute it would slide down over his left eye. The next minute it would be drifting past his ears toward the back of his head. More than once it became painfully aware to anyone who might be paying attention that beneath the flaming buttered steel wool on his head there was a conspicuously NSA style haircut. And haircuts like that are better suited to a cubicle in some office in downtown Los Angeles. It was just distracting enough to make him question his mission.

And he was just about to call it a mission impossible when a robe wearing man in dreadlocks emerged from the First Church of Rasta with something suspicious slung over his shoulder. Toole couldn't be sure, because it was in a canvas bag, but he thought it could be a rocket launcher. He was almost certain.

The man with the rocket launcher turned and walked toward Venice Beach unaware he was being followed by a soon-to-be stellar field agent for the NSA. Toole couldn't believe the man could be so brazen, so cavalier. He did his best to keep up with the robed man as he pursued him down the boardwalk, but it wasn't easy. Toole had never found himself in such a crowded setting among people wearing so little clothing. And they were all breathing. Some of them were breathing pretty heavily, and it was disturbing. Toole was no novice at listening to heavy breathing. That kind of heavy breathing by almost naked people could only mean one thing, and Tool seriously considered flagging a local law enforcement officer to report what he suspected.

After some thought however, Toole realized if he involved local law enforcement he would blow his cover. And he'd resolved to stay in character as long as it took to get the job done. Spotting that Rastafarian leaving the church with the rocket launcher had reminded him of how vitally important his mission was. Telling himself to focus on something other than the almost naked breathing people, he noticed how many men in board shorts there were on Venice Beach. For the first time he began to fear for the safety of the breathing people and their foreskins, especially the ones in board shorts. And robes.

Speaking of robes, where did the man with the rocket launcher go?

Following the intoxicating sound of oddly tropical music, Toole left the boardwalk and waded into the soft, deep sand of Venice Beach. Staying in the meager shadow of a palm tree, he held his breath as he spotted the Rastafarian and watched him unpack the canvas bag. With mixed feelings, he saw the man set up a kettle drum and join a group of other men in robes that were playing the kind of music he had only ever heard in ads for Carnival Cruise Lines.

He wasn't sure whether to be disappointed or relieved there was no rocket launcher. Or suspicious that the Rastafarians had taken him on a wild goose chase. What were they trying to keep him from? It had to be nearby, otherwise why distract him by leading him from the church to this nearby beach?

Walking slowly back to his car he thought hard about what might be nearby that would be important enough for the Rastafarians to keep him from. After opening the doors and windows to let the vinyl upholstery cool off before getting in, he leaned against the car and tried to concentrate. Out of the corner of his eye, a flash of red caught his attention. A man in a bright red satin yarmulke walked by and Toole knew it was no coincidence.

And just like that, he knew where he needed to go. The Israeli Consulate. It was only minutes away, on Wilshire Boulevard. And surely it would be teeming with men in robes. Possibly some very short men in robes.

But first he needed pudding. The plastic spoon

was burning a hole in his pocket and it was giving him an itch. And because all those almost naked people on Venice Beach breathing heavily made him think of Roz, it was an itch worse than the wig.

CHAPTER SIX

He seemed to come out of the mist that forever rises from the mountain. And although he often visited his grandsons, not once had he been compelled to wake them from their slumber and speak to them. Instead he would linger over them, shaping their dreams with tidbits he'd picked up among the clouds, or furthering their insights with flashes of inspiration from the ancestors.

But this was an auspicious moment. The time of the Wu was upon them.

"My grandsons, the oracle has spoken and it is time to awaken." His voice rang as a bell does in the thin mountain air out of the stillness of the night and into their dreaming minds. "The one we have waited for is found. The Wu has returned to human form in California, and it is your destiny to find her and return her to her rightful place. The world needs her now more than ever."

The old man had groomed his grandsons all their lives for this one task, as had been done each generation for three millennia. The Three knew there could be no undertaking more sacred. Each of them had an oracle bone from the ancient times around his neck, dangling from a simple cord made of braided hair from a yak's mane. On each was inscribed the task for which they were born:

Bring the Wu

"You must go to your uncle Fung Wah in Los Angeles. Tell him the ancestors have spoken and it is time to bring the Wu. And no matter what, do not let him ramble on endlessly until it silences your voices. As you know, his name means *great wind,* and it is no secret that he is known to blow on and on much like the inescapable wind. You must use all that I have taught you to contain him and use him wisely to your ends. Allow his wind to blow you in the direction of the Wu."

Although their grandfather had been with the ancestors since before they became men, all three knew he was not a man to be trifled with, especially in spirit form. So, despite the frigid night air among the clouds that cling to the sides of Wu Mountain, and despite the dark that wrapped its bat-like wings around them, they packed only what they knew they would absolutely need for the journey, and departed the simple home they had always known.

"You must listen for the sound of the bell, for it will lead you to the Wu."

His last words to them rang in their ears as they climbed down out of the clouds. On they walked, into the heart of the valley that would lead them past the three gorges of the Yangtze River. The brothers walked tirelessly and said little, each alone in his thoughts of the task ahead of them. They traveled to places they had never been, always following the ringing of the bell. Traveled through dense forests where the regal boughs of the pines sheltered them from the rains, and through wide valleys ringed by the Wu Mountains that faded far behind them as they pursued the persistent ringing of that bell.

Grandfather had told them with faith in the Wu and much perseverance they would find those who would see to it they reached their destination. And so it came to pass that three weeks after leaving Wu Mountain far behind, the bell did indeed lead them to safe passage across the water. As they sailed in grateful reverence for the depth and mystery of the ocean the Three spoke quietly about their plans, their uncle, and what they might see in America. And that, of course, led them to speak of the Wu.

Of course, when they slept they dreamed of pudding. Chocolate pudding. But that goes without saying.

There were the usual arguments about whether Grandfather had said the power of the Wu dates back to the Shang dynasty or the Zhou dynasty, but in the end it always came down to one simple fact: the dance of the Wu was timeless. It dated back to the very beginning of all that is.

She is the oldest and most powerful shamanic sorceress to have walked this earth. But the words shaman and sorceress are hardly suitable. Her beneficial power is not to be misunderstood or confused with the conjurers who brought the negative attention of governors and drew scorn. It was they who first began to banish the Wu and her dance for all time. Banished first of course was her communion with the invisible, the spirits who were drawn to her, blessing her with their omens. Always it was information she would collate and in turn, bless her people with.

It did not matter that she remained worthy of it at all times, remained steadfast in her virtue and faithful reporting of the visions. It did not matter that she was as much the message as she was the medium. Or perhaps it did matter. Perhaps that is what brought the wrath of emperors down upon her, for there has never been an emperor who was capable of remaining steadfast in the kind of virtue the Wu defined in her very being.

The celebration of the random was fated to leave this earth with the Wu. So with it was the dream interpretation, the knowledge of what will bring about healing, the clairvoyance, fortune telling, reversing of curses and banishing of unwanted spirits, and of course the invocations. The sacred prayers from the Wu were to be forbidden, done away with long before their grandfather was born. And the chilling stillness that gripped the hearts of the people when the dance of the Wu ended is still felt by many.

There is much discussion and debate about the usage of the word *dance* in relation to the Wu. It is strongly believed in the village from which the Three have come that it refers to the elegant and decidedly musical – in the way only a ringing bell can be – ongoing relationship the Wu has with the spirits. At any given time one or the other, Wu or spirit, may lead and the other follow as the dancers' graceful steps are inextricably woven into the fabric of life all around them. It is that dance which draws in the elements, divines meaning of dreams, brings healing insight to questions the seeker doesn't even know he has.

It is that decidedly musical ringing of the bell that

stirs the darkness from which the sleeper awakens. Upon awakening, the sleeper rises from the dream of separateness from all that is and all that ever has been or will be. It was the Wu who had mastered that ringing of the bell and celebration of the random and helped the people to realize and embrace their completeness.

But in the end it was the Confucian orthodoxy more than anything else that finalized her fate and worked tirelessly to banish and then outlaw the sacred powers of not just the Wu but women of that same nature, to stop the dance and limit them to a role of servitude.

That orthodoxy laid claim to power and authority by exhorting only the phallic ancestor cult which denied women representation of any kind in religion or the dance with spirits, seeing it as a threat to the lust so many men have for positions of man-made power in government office. Confucius and his cronies got prestige and status, and the Wu got burned in sacrifice along with her sisters, dancers with spirits and cripples that they were.

And just as soon as she was gone the prophecies began. In meditation the outlaw seer of visions, dreamer of dreams and healer of broken things would all learn and report back being given the same message: the Wu would return to them. But it would be a very long time, and when she did reappear it would be necessary to travel a great distance to escort her home. The Three, chosen by the ancestors long ago, bravest and most insightful among their generation, must find and bring the Wu.

And it just so happens that these three awakened by their grandfather's spirit were indeed the Three who were the bravest and most insightful of their generation. And it's a good thing because they were going to have to go to America. Everyone knows it takes a tremendous amount of courage and insight to go there.

There were many things the Three needed to learn once they arrived at their uncle's herb shop in Los Angeles. Among them was what their cover was for being there. But first, Fung Wah had to help them understand what he meant by *cover.* Far too patiently and in far too many words the good uncle explained that they were to pose as illegal organ traffickers because apparently being criminals in America was far preferable to pursuing noble deeds.

In America acquiring material wealth had somehow become conflated with the pursuit of noble deeds. And it was far easier to acquire material wealth as a criminal, since it was easier to blend in and not draw attention to oneself. Which is why all the politicians and religious leaders in America tend to dress alike and have the same haircuts. What difference is there really between the two? Both tell you what to think rather than risk the possibility you might learn how to think. Especially for yourself.

And so it was Fung Wah explained that what few people know about Chinese illegal organ traffickers is when they are working as operatives in the Unites States, they don't use their real names. There isn't a Chen or a Liu or a Xaio among them.

The Three needed to immerse themselves in American culture as both a means of blending in and of educating themselves about what is cherished most by the people of this great land they were visiting.

He explained they must choose names for themselves that are classic all-American names which will allow them to insert themselves into the culture without standing out. Names that reflect what they learned through careful study to be truly at the heart of the American people. So for weeks they immersed themselves in American culture. They watched television and movies, set up Twitter and Instagram accounts, watched YouTube videos and listened to talk radio while trying to make sense of the L.A. Times entertainment section.

At last the three found perfectly suitable new names because of how prominent those names were in all of it, and were pleased. Names that seemed to be revered and highly respected among the American people. Names that had demonstrated the fine art of smoke and mirrors, manipulation of facts, the sorcery of mesmerizing the people while committing crimes right before their eyes. Proving their uncle had been right: being a criminal was indeed the very best way to blend in.

And so it was that Pat Robertson, Bill O'Reilly and Dick Cheney left the Fung Wah Herb shop in Los Angeles at the end of those weeks fully prepared to bring the Wu. And though none of them could quite explain why because none of them had ever had it, all three were craving pudding. Chocolate pudding.

But immersing themselves in the cover story of being illegal organ traffickers took its toll on them as they ran errands for their good uncle which he would tell them were related to that detestable underground crime. It became harder and harder to know what was real and what was the legend, the role they were only playing. If ever there was a time for the dance of the Wu, it was now. If ever they needed a moment to celebrate the random, this was it.

They had all but forgotten their primary mission as

they drove up from Los Angeles to a place whose name evoked images of a beast of burden with a bad cold. And it annoyed them. But not nearly as much as seeing Pat Robertson get busted by the Oxnard Police. Dick Cheney was secretly relieved it had been Pat Robertson and not him though, considering what they'd seen on the internet about the many people who deeply wished to see Dick Cheney get busted. The things they said made him think if he did go to jail he would probably never get out.

They truly believed they were simply making a delivery to a patron of the illegal organ industry, much like the ones they had made for Fung Wah down in Los Angeles. As long winded as their uncle was, he had been surprisingly tight-lipped about the woman they were taking the curious powder to. And when things unfolded as they did, it took every ounce of insightful wisdom they had to not begin shooting at both the police and the woman when the bust went down. Had the two not been in the municipal parking lot seated in their uncle's car soothing their nerves with a simple breathing meditation when Constance Void and the woman wearing wallpaper came out of the police department, they might never have come to realize they had found what they were looking for.

Right up until they heard the bell summon the

demons that materialized from the smoke of the woman's firecracker, Bill O'Reilly and Dick Cheney thought their pursuit of the two women was just going to be another routine job of exacting vengeance like any illegal organ trafficker might find necessary in that line of work.

Until they heard her recite the incantation, they were certain they had been double crossed by yet another American woman pretending to be something she is not, for which eliminating the problem is considered the only solution to the Chinese. They are a people who despise deception and have no patience for con artists. It is simply beneath them.

But both recognized the firecracker as deeply meaningful due to its randomness. And it was that randomness that crawled up their spines and began tickling them behind the ears with a mockingbird feather. While some may be inclined to think of it as Operation Mockingbird, the two brothers thought only of having been tickled by the random.

As the smoke demons uncurled from around their feet in the Krispy Kreme parking lot and their eyes began to focus, they realized two things: they had been shooting at nothing but smoke, and Constance Void was the Wu. Their uncle confirmed their suspicions. In fact, he had sensed it the very first time she came into the Fung Wah Herb Shop. The signs were there. The dream about the mountain. The uncommon rains all spring. The woman's insistence she had heard about his shop through smoke signals. And every day for a week when he had thrown his I Ching he had gotten the hexagram for the Random.

He considered threatening to have their organs harvested as a punishment for letting the Wu get away but after not much thought and much bloviating Fung Wah ordered them to find her. It wasn't going to be easy, considering how powerful the magic of the Wu is. But first, they needed to get Pat Robertson out of jail; which proved to be much harder than any of them anticipated, largely because Pat Robertson discovered while he was there how much he enjoyed dancing with men and really wasn't sure he wanted to leave.

Bill O'Reilly secretly made a decision to ask the Wu, once they had retrieved her from behind her smoky curtain, for nothing more than exorcising the demons that had possessed Pat Robertson. Not because he'd discovered a fondness for dancing with men, but because he didn't seem to mind being in a jail cell in a town named after a beast of burden with a bad cold.

Neither he, nor Dick Cheney, looked forward to returning to the Oxnard jail to retrieve Pat Robertson, and especially disliked that they had to stay in Oxnard while awaiting word of his fate. Even though they had located the Wu, they had then lost her, which meant the entire trip had proven to be fruitless. But they did manage to find solace in the fact that they really didn't mind inhaling all that green smoke the Wu produced, and in fact looked forward to inhaling some more of it, even though it made them crave chocolate pudding.

CHAPTER SEVEN

"By the way, I got a smoke signal when I was out in the courtyard this morning. Your husband's received an email telling him you've gone to a convention out of the area and will see him next week." Constance was struggling to scoop a congealed lump of badly cooked, unappealing and no doubt tasteless oatmeal into a disposable plastic bowl. She started to reach for some fruit but upon inspection thought better of it because she strongly believed it was best not to eat anything that actually looked like waxed fruit.

Suzanne considered asking Constance if her husband had replied wanting to know why his wife hadn't contacted him herself. And who exactly was it who was claiming to have emailed him? Or for that matter how the mystery person had gotten his email in the first place. But she realized it would be feeding into her client's delusions to even respond. So instead she changed the subject and told Constance the director of the clinic had asked that she not practice any martial arts while at Pleasant Valley Sunday.

"It's disruptive. One patient is terrified of you already after seeing you in the courtyard this morning."

"If you're referring to the xenophobic pantheist, he's terrified of everything, including himself." While Suzanne couldn't disagree with her client's point, she repeated Dr. Carlson's request as she placed a bowl on her tray and reached for the serving spoon standing straight up in the oatmeal.

After trying to scoop some of the cereal into her bowl, she looked around self-consciously, unable to figure out how anyone managed to shake the gelatinous lump off the serving spoon. It seemed to be glued in place. She persisted, telling herself that if a bunch of alcoholics and crazy people could do it, she certainly could. When she finally gave it a firm enough shake to break the congealed lump free it went flying beyond the bowl and the tray it was on, an oatmeal wingless messenger of death. Most of the serving ended up on her stylishly out of place pumps. The Void thought it was actually an improvement on the general appearance of Suzanne's pumps but wisely did not say that out loud.

Instead, she excoriated the facility for serving hopelessly unhealthy institutional food to mental patients. "I mean, come on, diet has been proven to directly affect not just mood and health, but mental health. So why do they put the least amount of their budget into this low rent slop they're serving? And to make matters worse, they're serving it on disposable plastic. Do you know what this stuff is made of? Petroleum! What are they thinking? I realize they don't want to be sued by some family after a patient offs himself with a broken shard of ceramic or glass, but come on, there are ways to make sure that doesn't happen other than poisoning the patients with petroleum. And we both know all this plastic is just going to end up in the Great Pacific Garbage Patch."

Considering the astronomical fees Suzanne knew these institutions were bilking insurance companies for, she had to admit Constance was making a valid point. She also had to admit the banana she reached for did in fact look like it was waxed. The highly polished appearance of every piece of fruit available seemed to indicate they were all covered in petroleum based paraffin. Suzanne wondered why it was necessary for even the oranges, since oranges grew in abundance within minutes of the facility and wouldn't need any paraffin to preserve their freshness in transport. It simply made no sense.

"Nice to see your hair down, for a change."

Constance left the subject of petroleum contaminated food behind them as they crossed the dining room to an open table. "It's longer than I had thought it would be."

Suzanne smiled as she slid in across from Constance and told her once again about hair being the primary source of power in women. The longer the hair, the more centered a woman is in her power.

"Not necessarily just in women; in all people. Hair transmits subtle energy shifts in the atmosphere directly to the brain, not unlike the way an antenna transmits to a receiver. It was essential in the survival of early man who needed to know if a predator was approaching. And nothing says power like the ability to survive. But I am absolutely certain coating it with all that crap you put on yours pretty much negates any benefits your long hair might provide. So don't blame me when those Chinese sneak up on you in the middle of the night and steal your kidneys."

As Suzanne listened to Constance not just correct her but attempt to show more knowledge in the subject than she herself had, she made a mental note to inform Dr. Carlson that her client may need psychosurgery after all. For a woman in her client's position to think she may know more than a highly trained paid professional was without question delusional. But then again, so was thinking what they were attempting to eat was actually food. What she wouldn't give for a cup of chocolate pudding.

Lost in thought about pudding as she tried to swallow a bite of tasteless waxed banana, she was startled by the abrupt appearance of an emaciated man dressed in a crisp white shirt and red plaid bow tie slapping his tray down between her and Constance. Suzanne couldn't for the life of her figure out why he had bothered with a tray, since the only thing on it was a can of Boost liquid nutritional supplement.

"I see you've had a mishap with your pretty shoes. I have a link to a site that will help you restore them to looking new. I'll send it to your inbox. Are you set up for instant messaging yet?"

Mid-swallow, Suzanne could only blink. Unsure of what the young man was talking about, she shot Constance a furtive glance. Constance gently patted the young man's shoulder.

"Yes, that would be nice, Jerry."

Jerry had begun doing online social networking when his grandmother gave him a laptop for his twelfth birthday, and by his early twenties he was absolutely convinced he was in fact living online. Unable to distinguish between IRL and URL, he wandered in a confused haze, often claiming that he'd caught a virus and needed to defrag.

His family had grown concerned when they noticed he had stopped eating, mistaking his symptoms for a classic case of anorexia nervosa. When he was hospitalized for dehydration and it was learned he had lost thirty percent of his body weight, the doctors there insisted on in-patient treatment at a mental health facility since his condition was beyond their expertise. He reluctantly opened the can of Boost and took a sip, wincing and shaking his head in disgust at the excess sugar.

Jerry had tried explaining to the doctors that he had perfected a variation of sun-eating, where he absorbed pure energy from living on the internet, but that only made them more concerned that his self-starvation had affected his cognition, resulting in psychosis.

Constance smiled warmly. "Jerry is my favorite person here. We both have a wireless connection."

"I'm sorry. I'm being rude to your visitor. I should know better than to attempt to engage contact without first sending a friend request." He awkwardly extended his hand to Suzanne, who reluctantly took it in an equally awkward handshake.

"Jerry Fletcher. Twenty-two. Thousand Oaks. Online puzzle based games, social networking, movies, music, and stand-up comedy. Willing to do peer-to-peer file sharing with Linux operating systems only. No spam or porn, please."

"Zann." Suzanne said her name absently, distracted by a woman standing at the window. "Zann Killjoy, LMFT. Thousand Oaks."

"See? We've learned we have something in common already. Thousand Oaks."

But Suzanne's attention was focused on the woman at the window. She appeared to be wearing a sleeveless tee shirt with the letters SSDD on it. Suzanne had no idea what that meant, but that wasn't nearly as confusing as her hair situation. Not only did she have the thickest head of long disheveled hair Suzanne had ever seen, she also had what curiously appeared to be armpit hair tattoos to match. The woman stood pointing at the facility's resident feral cat who was trying to sneak up on a bird's nest in the courtyard's only tree. The cat had gotten halfway up the trunk and then froze, as if it sensed it was being watched.

"That's Glenn. Glenn Greenworld. 48. Moorepark. Superhero. Vanquishes corruption and all forms of evil by pointing at it."

Wide eyed, the cat seemed unable to shake the sense that it was under scrutiny and jumped down from the trunk of the tree. Constance nodded and smiled knowingly at Jerry.

"Looks like you and I aren't the only ones with a wireless connection." Suzanne wished Constance would stop saying that, largely because she had no idea what the Void meant by it.

"I'll shoot you a link about the work being done in Ventura County to mitigate the problem with feral cats through catch and release after vaccinating and neutering or spaying. It may take some time to find though because I've got way too many things bookmarked."

While Glenn Greenworld had always had the superpower of pointing at things, it wasn't until she experienced a freak industrial accident while working under the table at a candle factory that she began using it to point at corruption and injustice, the two true evils in this world. It began, in fact, when she woke in the hospital to discover she had no body hair. With the exception of the impossible crow's nest on top of her head, Glenn looked like she'd spent a week at some spa for women who always do what the fashion industry tells them to do.

When she got the hospital bill she took it to her employer, who fired her immediately. So she called the California Department of Employment to lodge a complaint and was told her employer had been running his operation under the radar and had no Worker's Compensation Insurance. It was up to her to pay the bill in full. When she asked if the employer would be charged with anything or lose his business license, it was explained to her the investigation and prosecution of businesses operating within the *underground economy* ordinarily comes out of the state's discretionary fund, but discretionary funds are always the first thing to disappear during hard economic times.

She looked at all the corruption going on around her and couldn't help but notice it was always the people at the bottom of the ladder who were being sacrificed for the comforts of those at the top. There didn't seem to be many prosecutions of those at the top, especially those in government.

So she did what any self-respecting woman in her position would do: she tore up the hospital bill, kissing her good credit goodbye along with any chance of renting anything in a decent neighborhood again, and moved to Little Tijuana off Oxnard Boulevard. Then she took the last of her savings and went to the best tattoo artist in Ventura County. When she asked him to give her armpit hair tattoos it confused him at first. He thought she wanted something colorful and unique tattooed in her armpits. It was a popular look. But she just shook her head and pointed to the crow's nest.

"See this shit on my head? I want armpit hair tattoos that look like this shit. Got it?"

The tattoo artist nodded and gave Glenn Greenworld exactly what she wanted. By the time she left his shop she had three tangled crow's nests; one on her head and two under her arms. Then she started standing outside the Ventura County Courthouse in sleeveless shirts pointing at judges, attorneys, prosecutors and other officers of the court. Largely because they're the ones who serve the interests of the politicians and their corporate handlers with public funds and she was sick of it.

While at first it had no effect whatsoever, it wasn't long before a number of judges discovered when it came time to make rulings they knew to be questionable, they were unable to. Inexplicably, it was as though the ruling was stuck in their throat. Frozen. And because Ventura County has such a large Hispanic population, and Hispanics can be quite superstitious, the judges who experienced the curious malady concluded the woman who pointed outside the courthouse was putting some kind of voodoo hex on them.

Glenn Greenworld was given a cease and desist order by the court which forbid her from coming within five hundred feet of the courthouse. So she started standing outside public schools and school board meetings, having neither forgotten nor forgiven the transgressions of corrupt administrators she had struggled with when attempting to extract an actual education for her children.

In time, the County of Ventura had no choice but to declare the woman who points to be a hazard to herself and others. She had been the longest resident in the history of the Pleasant Valley Sunday Rehabilitation and Psychiatric Treatment Center, and Constance was concerned about what the food there was doing to the poor unfortunate superhero.

"So are you one of the new doctors here, Zann?" Jerry had to ask, having grown accustomed to seeing doctors come and go with regularity in his time at the rehabilitation center.

"Not really. I'm here for Con....Morgan. But I do have my own office to use for as long as she needs inpatient treatment here at the clinic." Suzanne realized she needed to spend some time practicing their new names after stumbling over the one Constance had chosen. And Constance realized Suzanne had scored somewhere safe to sleep at night, which meant she was better at hiding from Chinese illegal organ traffickers than she had expected the court appointed therapist to be.

"After meeting her last night I did a search on Morgan La Fay and learned some interesting things."

Suzanne's heart sank. She hadn't been aware that her client had used a name that was common enough to be found on the internet. What if Dr. Carlson found out and asked her about it? Then she realized that the patient telling her he'd found the name on the internet was delusional, and relaxed. None of the patients had access to the internet at the clinic. Before he could launch into what he'd learned about Morgan La Fay, he noticed a man in wrinkled khaki slacks and a torn yellowed tee shirt enter the courtyard and light a cigarette.

"Oh look, it's Jack Kerouac."

Jerry was obviously eager to leave the table and join the smoking man. He waved for a staff member to come verify that he had finished the can of Boost while he explained what he'd learned about Jack Kerouac on the internet earlier. Suzanne just shook her head sadly and engaged in active listening the best she could.

"First of all, Kerouac didn't exactly die from a bleeding ulcer like the papers claimed. Depending on what conspiracy theorist website you go to, his death had to do with any one of a number of things. Women, mainly. You know how writers are. But also there's something about macaroni. And a bad fall down some stairs, but I'm not sure if it was because he was drunk or slipped on some macaroni. It gets confusing. Best advice I can give is look it up for yourself. But don't get bogged down by that persistent myth that he didn't die at all, which is why the Gap went to so much trouble to airbrush those pictures of him modeling their khakis. I almost fell for that one myself."

Suzanne was finding it harder and harder to engage in active listening with Jerry and truly wished he hadn't mentioned macaroni because now that was all she could think about. That and chocolate pudding. And why would the clinic let a patient admit himself under the obviously assumed name of Jack Kerouac?

A staff member carrying a clipboard with authority came and shook the can of Boost to find that it was indeed empty. After making a note with equal authority he nodded to Jerry that he was free to go. As Jerry stood to rush to the door, he explained his excitement.

"Jack's working on a pitch for a reality TV show, and he says if they turn it down I can produce it for him as a web series!"

Constance felt it was only right that she explain two things to Suzanne: the man in the courtyard was not in fact Jack Kerouac. It was just a nickname he'd earned in college because he majored in creative writing and liked drinking booze out of an empty pill bottle he used as a shot glass. His real name was John. But nobody called him that.

"At least, I think it's John. I'm having a little trouble pinning him down on that, which isn't at all uncommon considering why he's here." John was just another garden variety alcoholic writer who thought being drunk all the time was necessary in order to be any good at his craft.

"And the second thing?" Suzanne wondered just how her client managed to learn so much about the patients in the few hours they'd been there, especially considering their late arrival the night before.

"He wants a reality TV show for writers where nothing happens. All they do is sit at a typewriter and stare at a blank piece of paper. He thinks it will give readers a more realistic idea of what writers actually do. And Jerry wants to be involved in the production because he thinks it may help him transition away from an electronic screen to something more tangible he can actually touch."

"Like what, paper?"

She wondered if the man had drunk himself into deliriums, since everyone knows writers no longer use typewriters and paper. They have word processing programs and the cloud. But she did admire Jerry's instincts in thinking work might help him return to the very human life going around them all, the one in which people actually eat food.

As she watched Jerry join the man whose name might possibly be John, she noticed the woman who points step out into the courtyard and aim her finger at the ground in front of them. It didn't take long for both John and Jerry to see that she was pointing at cigarette butts and for John to begin picking them up. Jerry helped out by doing a search on the topic and learning that cigarette butts are toxic to birds, who tend to think they're food. Suzanne sincerely hoped Jerry didn't get it stuck in his head that cigarette butts actually were food.

"There's one of the patients who had the same dream I had last night."

Suzanne had been lost in thought about food, perhaps as an escape from the food-like products on the tray that sat staring at her like the ugly kitten at the pet shop everybody knows full well it isn't going to get adopted. Not because it's ugly, but because it can't help but bite and scratch, much like institutional food does as it's going down.

But now she was remembering Constance saying something about dreaming of chocolate pudding and leaf blowers, and was again relieved she had the lab coat to cover the mysterious stains on her Laura Ashley dress.

"How is it even possible for two people to have the same dream? Isn't it more likely that they were watching the same television program just before going to bed and images from it emerged during their dreams that were similar enough to make it seem like they had the same dream?"

Constance smiled and patiently reminded Suzanne that she doesn't watch television, then explained Haj hadn't watched any television the night before either, having long since learned the whole business of passive entertainment was unsettling to him. While he wasn't as empathic as the Void, he was far too sensitive for the assault to the senses that television can be.

"Otherwise, your argument would be a sound one. Isn't that why they call it *programming*?"

"So does Haj have a theory about what's behind your identical dreams?" Suzanne pushed her tray away and leaned back in her chair, wanting chocolate pudding more than ever. She hadn't said anything about her own dream the night before and didn't intend to. It would only be playing into her client's hand.

"He thinks it's the Jinni." Constance nodded toward the dark-skinned man carrying a tray of food-like products, who returned the nod. She pointed to the chair next to her, but he shook his head, making it clear he wanted to eat alone. She understood, but wasn't sure Suzanne ever would. A good Muslim man dining alone with two women to whom he was neither married nor related was something that was beneath his character.

"A Jinni is a supernatural being in the Islamic faith. What we westerners would call a Genie."

"A Genie?" Suzanne sounded incredulous. "How can anyone in this day and age believe in something like that, something so...superstitious?"

Constance sat quietly for a few moments contemplating the irony in Suzanne's statement before she continued.

"The Jinni is nothing like the character Robin Williams played the voice of in that Disney movie. Nor is it like the one Barbara Eden played on television, popping out of a bottle in a skimpy outfit and granting wishes. The Jin is much more closely related to what you might refer to as a demon. Evil thoughts and deeds are often attributed to them in Islamic lore."

Suzanne was stopped short by the mention of demons. She knew better than anyone else how easy it was for demons to plant thoughts in people's heads that lead them astray. While she wanted nothing more than a good robust theological discussion right then and there, it didn't seem prudent to have it with her client. So instead she asked Constance what had brought Haj to the Pleasant Valley Sunday Rehabilitation and Psychiatric Treatment Center.

Constance explained that Haj had grown convinced a Jin was infiltrating his thoughts after he began hearing a voice that was not his own and obviously not of this world telling him terrible things.

"Terrible things?" Suzanne was alarmed. Images of exploding buildings and planes falling from the sky in flames flashed through her mind as she fought the urge to look under the table for a terrorist bomb.

"Telling him he is unworthy, unloved, unnecessary to his god, his family, his world. These unbearable messages have driven the dear man from a position of respect in his profession and his Mosque, as well as honorable and beloved head of his family, to one of despair and self-loathing. But curiously, they initially started out telling him to commit horrible acts of violence against others, which he steadfastly refused to do."

They were the same terrible things Suzanne had heard her own clients tell her they were hearing from the voices in their heads, with the same effect. She wondered if Haj was one of the clients Dr. Carlson was considering doing psychosurgery on, and hoped to see the doctor later so she could ask him. She also wondered if every culture in the world had a name for those demons that possess and torment those who are vulnerable to it.

And it wasn't hard to make oneself vulnerable to it. Suzanne remembered a classmate she'd known at Evangelical University, and how she'd gone on to establish a clinical practice in Seattle after graduation, relying heavily on exorcism for her patients. Unfortunately, she did it without taking the necessary precautions and ended up possessed herself. Proximity to those demons will do it every time. It wouldn't surprise her to learn that some patients at Pleasant Valley Sunday had become possessed merely by sitting next to a possessed patient in the cafeteria or while watching television in the day room, especially if they had made themselves vulnerable to it by engaging in certain unholy activities.

Suzanne considered what she knew about the two people who had the same dream. One smoked the devil weed, practiced voodoo, and opened herself up to demonic possession by communing with questionable spirits. The other devoutly worshiped a religion that was neither Christian nor adhered to a literal interpretation of the Bible, which clearly sets its followers up for demonic possession, no matter how

112

well-meaning they may be. Considering both had pretty obvious similarities in the elements that would attract demons, Suzanne was fairly certain the third person Constance mentioned having had the same dream would be similar in some way.

Perhaps it was the xenophobic pantheist, which would not surprise her at all. Pantheism was a spiritual disaster waiting to happen, leaving the human soul nothing more than one huge walk-in closet for the devil and his minions to move into and unpack their unholy designer shoe collections. She looked around for Carlos, but didn't see him in the dining room or the courtyard, and wondered if it had anything to do with having had the same dream as the others.

"You mentioned a third person dreamed about chocolate pudding and leaf blowers last night. Who are they, and what can you tell me about them?"

"I think you know that already, Suzanne." Constance locked her in a tractor beam disguised as eye contact. It was inescapable.

"After all, that other person is you."

Suzanne had to admit, it was pretty random. So why didn't she feel like celebrating?

Constance on the other hand wasn't exactly celebrating the random. She'd been distracted by a train of thought ever since the issue of demons started being tossed around, and in the absence of any TrainWreck was unable to get any feedback on it via smoke signal. While she was certain demons weren't behind what was going on at Pleasant Valley Sunday, she was equally certain shenanigans were. From everything Constance Void had come to know about them, where there are shenanigans, it's more likely there are *daemons* behind it. Those silent little unobtrusive devils. Shenanigans for sure.

CHAPTER EIGHT

Toole drove to Wilshire Boulevard in West Los
Angeles and sat parked across the noisy, smog-choked
boulevard from the Federal building. He recalled the
crowd of protesters he had surveilled months earlier
and the heavily fortified LAPD officers who escorted
them to the Israeli Consulate. There hadn't been a
single man in a robe among them. *Was it because they
were just dressing like everyone else to blend in?* He
hadn't considered that as a possibility and it made him
realize he had much to learn on the road to becoming a
stellar field agent.

Either way, he knew he would need to leave the
safe duck blind of his car and go on foot from there to
get close enough to the consulate to see anything of
importance. And that was a problem. He was still in his
Venice Beach disguise, which was entirely unsuitable
for Wilshire Boulevard. He needed to change into the
other costume he'd picked up at the rental shop, and

there wasn't anywhere to do that but the duck blind, and that just wouldn't do.

How did Superman do it? And more importantly, how did Superman change clothes in a phone booth without anyone noticing there was a grown man in a phone booth changing into red pajamas and a cape?

His mind seemed to be stuck on that question until it occurred to him it didn't matter. There are no phone booths on Wilshire Boulevard anyway. With the advent of cell phones, they became irrelevant. If it wasn't for the astronomical fees certain predatory telecommunication companies were able to get from prisoners and their families for phone service in American correctional institutions, there would be nothing resembling a pay phone in America anymore. Such is progress, especially for predatory telecommunication companies.

As he sat there considering awkwardly changing out of the bell bottoms, suede fringe jacket and vest right there in the car, it occurred to Toole what he really needed was a restroom. And pudding. Chocolate pudding. Realizing he wasn't far from Fairfax Avenue and the best Jewish deli on the west coast, he checked his watch. It was the lunch hour. Canter's would be swamped with people lining up for their Reuben

116

sandwiches and black & white cookies that aren't really cookies at all. No one would notice his change of appearance if he used their restroom and then got in line wearing his disguise. He could taste the chocolate pudding already, and knew for fact it really was chocolate pudding.

Since all they had at the costume shop that seemed appropriate for the situation was costumes for Fiddler on the Roof, Toole had to settle for a long tunic-like black coat with no lapels rather than the full length black robe he'd envisioned. Coupled with black slacks, uncomfortable black shoes and a black fedora with a beard attached to it, he had to admit he'd done a pretty good job once he saw himself in the mirror. Hastily applying a dab more spirit gum to that spot where he'd never been able to grow sideburns, he wished he'd had a bit more time to secure the beard before someone began knocking on the restroom door.

The problem of course was late spring in Southern California often sees temperatures into the mid to upper eighties, and the costume was made of polyester. Few people understand polyester is made out of petroleum, and Toole was allergic to petroleum. To make matters worse, the beard was also polyester. By the time the customer in line ahead of him had placed his order, Toole was doing the "Itchy dance." It was similar to the one he'd been doing in Venice, only it wasn't isolated to just his head. His whole body was digging the beat.

As if the universe itself had decided to send him back-up, a wave of relief swept over him when he noticed something as he ordered. While the pretty girl at the counter wrote down his request for chocolate pudding, that enigmatic universe that Bill Nye the Science Guy still insists is not an omniscient being turned Toole's attention to a signed framed photograph of Guns n' Roses on the wall behind her.

"Welcome to the Jungle!"

Axl Rose's signature scrawled in black Sharpie across the bottom gave Toole just the encouragement he needed to go on despite the discomfort, knowing that only the most stalwart of stellar field agents could possibly pass this kind of test. The jungle just isn't for everybody. And the mysteriously coded messages from the universe obviously aren't for Bill Nye the Science Guy.

Spotting an open seat at a table for two at the front window, Toole worked his way to it and made brief eye contact with the woman seated there, who nodded for him to sit down. He knew better than anyone how risky it was for someone in the NSA to make eye contact with an actual breathing person. He also knew it was the kind of thing that was a judgment call in the field. Toole was a man of action who was quickly learning to think on his feet. Sliding into the seat across from her, he had just taken his first bite of the perfect chocolaty kosher delight when the brazen woman took liberties with the eye contact they had already established and spoke out loud with actual words.

"Surely that's not all you're having for lunch."

She said it in a tone that would have sounded motherly to him if Toole knew what that tone actually sounded like. His own mother had never been the motherly type.

"You're going to need something more substantial than that to keep your energy up for your performance."

Performance? Toole's heart sank. Mossad was on to him already. He'd only been there a few minutes and they'd not only spotted him, they'd sent someone to make sure he knew they were on to his disguise. The spoonful of chocolate pudding in his mouth expanded in size to take up every bit of space and then some. It became the chocolate pudding equivalent of the Big Bang in his mouth and entire galaxies were forming.

If Bill Nye had been there he might have pointed out its obvious lack of omniscience. As it became a black hole sucking his confidence into it, it began to work its way down the back of his throat and threaten to cut off his air supply. There's no oxygen in space, and Toole blamed Bill Nye. The woman brazenly continued. This time it was a question.

"So what part are you playing?"

Part? His thoughts raced. *What part would the NSA be playing in an operation like this? The most important one, of course! But how did Mossad find out? And when had they begun tailing him? Was it back on Venice Beach, or before that even?*

His mind raced as he jumped from thought to thought like some kid with ADHD playing tag with a live hand grenade.

"How did you know?"

He swallowed finally and took a sharp breath, giving the woman the best steely gaze he could muster. There may not be oxygen in space but as long as there was oxygen here he had no intention of letting Mossad keep him from it. Or from pudding. He was sure Bill Nye would approve. Or at least reluctantly agree.

The woman gave him a satisfied smile and leaned back in her chair. Her smugness made him want to stab himself in the thorax with the spoon. Or maybe her thorax. Either way, he definitely wanted to do some spoon stabbing of a thorax. In the end, he realized there was more to be gained by playing it cool and finding out how much Mossad knew, so he just stabbed the pudding, which had no thorax so he stabbed it in the chocolate. Somewhere in a parallel not-at-all omniscient universe, Bill Nye is watching an episode of Law and Disorder wherein the pudding did it but gets off after proving it was self-defense.

"The rest of the cast has been coming in for lunch all week. But you must be the understudy, because it's the first time I've seen you. Besides, today's your opening day. Nobody but the understudy has time for lunch on opening day. Am I right?"

He followed her eyes as she nodded toward the door and for the first time noticed the poster taped to it. Fiddler on the Roof was opening that evening at the Performing Arts Center. And as is often the case with musicals, the final dress rehearsal was open to senior citizens and the disabled that afternoon. Also noticing for the first time the woman's cane leaning up against the side of the table and the playbill next to her coffee cup, he smiled knowingly. Toole wanted to tell himself it was just a coincidence, but his not at all motherly mother had always said anyone who believes in coincidence just isn't paying attention.

He winked at the woman and smiled. "This is my lucky pudding. Last time I ate it before the opening,

the lead actually did break a leg and I got his part."
The woman let out a motherly laugh and Toole
congratulated himself on his quick thinking. Before the
two parted he told more than one lie and signed her
playbill, promising he'd blow her a kiss from the
wings. When she'd told him Fiddler on the Roof was
her favorite musical and she never missed a
performance, he was suspicious at first, naturally. The
song *Matchmaker?* Clearly a reference to matching
organ donors and recipients.

Still growing accustomed to the whole interacting
with actual real breathing people who make words
come out of their mouths thing, he thought carefully
about what he wanted to ask her next. The words just
would not come to him. His eyes kept going back and
forth between her hair and her face and something
about what he was seeing just didn't make sense to
him.

"I can tell you're the curious, observant type. So
why don't you ask me what it is you've been dying to
know?"

Toole wasn't sure if she'd put him at ease or simply
under more pressure. So he did his best, for what it was
worth. "I guess I was just wondering about you coming
here to eat and going to see Fiddler on the Roof. How
does that old joke go, 'funny you don't look Jewish?'

Except your hair. You've definitely got Jewish hair."
Toole hoped it didn't sound as awkward to her as it felt
saying it.

"You sir, are a delight," she laughed. "I've got to
remember that part about having Jewish hair. The girls
will love it!" She didn't answer his question, but he
realized later he hadn't really asked one.

A while later as he crossed Wilshire Boulevard
fortified with kosher chocolate pudding Toole had a
renewed confidence in his ability to carry out that
mission. He had managed to successfully blend in,
which meant he had achieved his goal of wearing a
convincing disguise, even if that disguise was clearly a
costume.

He approached the fountain in front of the Israeli
Consulate as he nonchalantly whistled *the Dream*. He
wasn't sure just why he'd chosen to whistle that rather
than *If I Were a Rich Man*, since that was the one most
recognizable from the musical. But considering his
primary objective: blazing a trail for those who dream
of being field agents for the NSA, it seemed to fit. At
least it wasn't *Matchmaker*. Considering the lucrative
illegal organ trafficking trade the Israelis were so
heavily invested in, whistling that song while sitting
outside the Israeli Consulate seemed like courting
disaster.

The mist created by the splashing fountain gave him cooling relief from the uncomfortable heat and itchy disguise as he sat at its edge and practiced using peripheral vision rather than look directly at the people coming and going from the consulate. It was somewhat disheartening for him to see the men entering and leaving wore stylishly modern business suits, and he was about to call the mission a bust when something caught his attention. The tiniest little person Toole had ever seen was being helped out of the building by another woman, and both were wearing robes.

If it had been Constance Void, she would have said it was a midget in a robe. For that matter, if it had been the Void, she would have been more accurate and said it was a midget in a sari. In fact, she would most likely have pointed and said *there go two women wearing saris, and one of them is a midget.* And what's more, being that the Void was not one to overlook details, especially in pointing things out, she would have correctly referred to the dot between their foreheads as a bindi.

But Constance Void was not there. The only one seated by the fountain just then was a would-be stellar field agent for the NSA, and since he still hadn't figured out how to send smoke signals, he decided to follow them. How else was he supposed to find out who they were and what they were doing with Mossad?

With his not-at-all motherly mother's words about coincidence ringing in his ears, Toole watched the two women approach a car parked just behind his own on Wilshire and get in. Without a moment to spare, he pulled away from the curb and eased into traffic, careful to stay several cars behind them. Agent Toole knew following them was going to pay off big time. Not just for him, but for all stellar NSA field agents to come. And of course for his country.

He was not one bit surprised or disappointed to see they were headed for Pasadena, home of Cal Tech. Something told him this case was bigger than anything even he had suspected. Cal Tech was not just the source of much of the technology the NSA was using, it was also the source of many of their top analysts. He should know. Toole was one of them. It wouldn't surprise him to learn his alma mater was also the source of much of who and what Mossad had at their disposal as well. The plot thickened. Maybe not as thick as pudding, but thick enough to know he had to keep his wits about him.

As it turned out, the largest Hindu temple in Southern California is also in Pasadena, and that was where the two unusual women were headed. He sat outside the temple playing with the knobs of his car radio while absolutely nothing happened far too long before deciding the two may have been leading him to Pasadena for some reason other than the Hindus. It took every ounce of focus he was capable of to come up with what the connection was.

And then it hit him: The Catholics. He'd been wrong to assume the Los Angeles Archdiocese was involved. No one was better than the Catholics at diverting attention from themselves by playing the shell game with key players in criminal conspiracies.

La Salle High School is in Pasadena, and it's run by the Christian Brothers. Toole honestly didn't know why he hadn't thought of it sooner. Of course both Catholic priests and students would be involved. Not only do priests wear robes, but nobody is easier to radicalize than adolescent boys.

Not only were teenage boys the perfect fall guys, but the media never seems to look beyond their video games, music or mental health history for a more plausible explanation for their carnage. Toole found himself wishing he had the soundtrack to Fiddler on the Roof so he could listen to *the Dream* on repeat as he headed east on Sierra Madre Boulevard, certain he was on the right track. He had to be. The midget had sent him.

It turned out to be harder than he'd anticipated to park where he could watch the school surreptitiously. Both the parking lot and side streets were jammed with parked cars, and it took a while before Toole remembered La Salle's graduation was earlier than other schools. As he circled the building searching for any spot that might be open, he absently switched on the radio and chuckled when *Just Like Tom Thumb's Blues* came over the rock station he'd landed on. Wasn't Tom Thumb a midget? Correcting himself, he glanced in the rear view mirror and apologized to his more critical self.

Little person.

Circling the block was getting Toole nowhere, and having arguments with himself about midgets in rock & roll songs was all the proof he needed. It was time to rethink his approach. Reluctantly, he finally decided to pay yet another exorbitant city parking fee and leave the long jacket with the hat and beard in the car. It only made sense to him that he would better blend in at a Catholic high school dressed in just the white shirt and black slacks, especially when he pulled his necktie and sport coat out of the trunk.

Rather than take a seat, he lingered in the back of the auditorium because it allowed him to see everyone who came and went without having to draw attention to himself. It seemed at first to be a waste of time as first one Brother then another stood at the podium and bored the eager young men to tears. But then something happened Toole could never have expected. Navy Admiral Thomas Thumbsen received a standing ovation from the ROTC graduates in the class as he stood and approached the podium.

It could not be a coincidence. Toole didn't need a weather man to know which way the wind blows, and he certainly didn't need his mother to tell him to pay attention to the not-at-all coincidental coincidences that had stacked up and pointed him in this direction like jumbo jets waiting to land at LAX.

Or a midget.

A Navy Admiral was the equivalent to a general. Tom Thumb, the midget, had been a general. And Admiral Thomas Thumbsen's command post was none other the Air Naval base at Point Mugu, one of the nuclear armed bases in none other than Ventura County.

The NSA analyst in his logic center sat back, put his feet up on the desk, and popped the foil top off a fresh cup of pudding. Instinctively, Toole reached down and felt for the plastic spoon still in his pocket, smiling.

CHAPTER NINE

Bill O'Reilly and Dick Cheney spent the night on Silver Strand Beach in nearby Port Hueneme sleeping off all the chocolate pudding they had binged on at Peggy's All Night Diner and Laundromat on Channel Islands Boulevard. As the brothers had spent their lives hand washing their clothing at a mountain spring near their humble home, it surprised them that in America people could throw their laundry into a machine at any hour of the day or night and eat entertaining food while the machine did the work for them.

While the euphoria from that much chocolate made sleeping on Silver Strand seem like a good idea at the time, had it not been for the ringing of the cell phone their good uncle had given Bill O'Reilly, they might have gotten hypothermia. An icy fog had settled in during the night and soaked their hair and clothing. Their waitress had called it *June Gloom,* which seemed odd to them because it was still May.

But Port Hueneme has a climate that is different from that of most of Southern California. Its beach lies along the Santa Barbara Channel, which forms a funnel that seems only to bring in either a chilling wind or icy fog to the residents of the little city whose other three sides share a border with the city of Oxnard. By the time they heard the ringing phone and realized what it was, the frigid morning wind had begun to stir the fog and chill Bill O'Reilly and Dick Cheney to the bone. Sitting up, Bill O'Reilly spat twice and flipped open the phone.

"Uncle, you have news?"

His sandy voice was weak from the chocolate hangover.

"Yes. Their forensic lab has determined the substance the Oxnard Police took from your brother last night was in fact powdered ginseng and not human testes. Pat Robertson is free to go. But there is a problem. He refuses to leave unless we bail out someone he spent the night dancing with."

The good uncle was wiring the money for the young dance partner's bail to a place called Lucky Grocery on Channel Islands Boulevard not far from where they were. Bill O'Reilly and Dick Cheney saw it as provident and knew the ancestors were smiling down on them. What could be more fortunate than picking up money at a lucky grocery store?

And when they paid the bail for their brother's dance partner and learned he might have been arrested for something having to do with green smoke, both men were pleased with Pat Robertson for his wise choice in dance partners. They also thought it significant that his eyes were the same grayish-green color as the smoke the Wu had created with her mystical conjuring in the Krispy Kreme parking lot the night before.

Smokey Methson, a blend of Philippino, German, Samoan and Hispanic ancestry was typical of the sons and daughters of Port Hueneme. But he preferred to call himself a Planetarian. He was the invariable product of generations of U.S. sailors returning with their brides from every port of call where America has stationed itself in its many empire building pursuits around the globe. Over the decades their children have intermarried and produced the perfect definition of multiculturalism: a place where just about every culture of the world has been put on a revolving dance floor whose control switch got stuck on high and couldn't be stopped. There is no food, no music, no lyrical language to be found anywhere like it in America. And can those people dance.

As Smokey explained every detail of his origins

except for his arrest, Pat Robertson listened dreamily to the sound of his voice, tapping his foot to a beat which seemed to be discernible to only the two dancers in the back seat. Before Dick Cheney could steer them into traffic that would be intractable on the 101 that time of day, the young man with impossibly elegant cheekbones advised him to take Pacific Coast Highway instead.

Although it was unlike Dick Cheney to avoid getting himself and others into anything intractable, Bill O'Reilly sternly reminded him it was important to listen to the voice of reason, especially if it was someone who was more familiar with the terrain and therefore knew what they were talking about. When that didn't work he reminded them they were in America, where democracy rules and he was outvoted.

"Your brother has explained what the three of you are doing here, and I would like to help in any way I can." The expert American dancer gazed into Pat Robertson's eyes as he spoke and it seemed a foregone conclusion he and Pat Robertson would be joined at the hip for the duration of their stay in California. Bill O'Reilly sighed heavily as he and Dick Cheney briefly made eye contact. Both men could only hope when they returned to the Fung Wah Herb Shop in Los Angeles their good uncle could resist the temptation to bloviate about the historical origin of men dancing together dating back to ancient China.

Having been told about finding and then losing the Wu by Bill O'Reilly while on the phone the night before, and a few more details that morning, Fung Wah jumped into action, knowing there was no time to spare. They needed the expert tracking skills of some good hackers. The only thing Fung Wah had mastered on the internet was downloading word porn, where uncommonly verbal porn stars talk over each other until achieving climax and then fall asleep.

As much as he detested doing it, he knew he would need to contact the actual real Chinese illegal organ traffickers because of their close involvement with the Chinese government. Everyone knows the Chinese government has the best computer hackers on the planet, and it would take the best to locate the Wu. The risk of course was that the atheist Chinese government would consider the Wu a threat, much the same way they consider Falun Gong to be, and harvest her organs as a way of silencing her the same way they do with them. But not before conveniently labeling them *dissidents*.

Smokey Methson proved to be more of a help than any of them had anticipated. In a curious twist of fate he had been misdirected to the wrong courtroom and was actually sitting there watching as Constance Void was found in contempt and sentenced to court appointed therapy with a woman dressed in wallpaper. Having the name of the other woman would be essential in putting a trace on them, even if it did leave all but Smokey unsure of just why he was at the courthouse that day.

It only made sense to Fung Wah that they would begin by looking closely at all treatment centers where Suzanne Shill had admitting privileges. It seemed to him hiding in one would be a perfect cover. But after exhaustive research and detective work, the information their contacts in the Chinese government obtained proved useless. No one by either name had been admitted or done any admitting.

He started thinking he may need to send his nephews back up to Ventura County to personally question the admitting staff in every treatment center there. But Dick Cheney surprised them all by having an idea that might actually save a lot of effort, money, and time spent intractably stuck somewhere. It was the kind of surprise that took everyone a moment to recover from.

"Why don't we look for new patients with names that sound like men? And also for who admitted them. If both therapist and patient have a man's name, it would be worth looking more closely."

He was watching Smokey and Pat Robertson dance among the shelves lined with jars of dried herbs when the idea came to him.

Fung Wah was pleased. He could see his nephews had been taught well. After placing a call to his contacts, he suggested they all go out for something to eat while they wait to hear back from them. Unfortunately for the good uncle and Smokey Methson, the others insisted they find somewhere that served chocolate pudding. They both would have much preferred to dine on pork Chow Yun-Fat smothered in barbecue sauce followed with sticky buns at the Shanghai Noodle Factory up the street. Especially Smokey, who was pleased to discover he was developing a taste for Chinese.

By the time they left the noisy far too brightly lit family restaurant with its red and white checkered curtains and matching tablecloths they had unfinished patty melts in Styrofoam to-go containers under their arm and a text message from their contact. He had two possible leads which seemed promising. A man named Joseph Smith had admitted a patient named Ron Hubbard in Moorepark, and a patient named Morgan La Fay had been admitted by someone named Zann Killjoy.

Smokey proved to be helpful once again, which tickled Pat Robertson. He pointed out that Morgan La Fay had been the name of a sorceress in the time of King Arthur's court, and because he had seen the wallpapered woman in action, thought Killjoy would certainly be a fitting pseudonym for the therapist they were looking for.

After very little discussion, even from their ordinarily long-winded uncle, they all dismissed the other two names because they sounded too lacking in creative thought to be anything other than the names of typically unimaginative American men, the kind of men who decide to start a religious cult because it's easier to fleece people than it is to get a job. They agreed without hesitation to focus on the facility in Camarillo and see what they could find out about the sorceress and her killjoy therapist.

To that end, Fung Wah once again reached out to his contact with the organ traffickers, who told him he had located an oddly wallpapered Cadillac in Camarillo registered to Suzanne Shill, and its back windows had been shot out. Biting his tongue to keep himself from tipping his hand, the aging herbalist gently persuaded him to learn as much as he could about the facility in Camarillo for him without actually explaining why.

The trick to asking favors of Chinese illegal organ traffickers is to put oneself in the position where they owe you, a position which the herbalist had carefully cultivated over the years. Nobody is more aware of how necessary it is to keep one's organs in the best of health than those who routinely traffic in them illegally. Fung Wah's herbs are known on three continents for their value in supporting good organ health.

As well, the growing concern about the extinction of the rhinoceros had been leading many to seek an alternative aphrodisiac to the creature's coveted horn, and no herbalist on the planet produced a more effective alternative than Fung Wah.

Of course what the herbalist didn't tell any of them was the secret ingredient is the synthetic rhino horn he gets from the biotech firm his San Francisco contacts connected him with. Those geeks figured out how to create them on a 3D printer using rhino DNA, and it didn't surprise Fung Wah one bit. It was San Francisco, after all.

In fact, had the good uncle bothered to look beyond his limited selection of word porn sites, he would have discovered there is a whole genre of pornography inspired by his most effective aphrodisiac concoction. Known as *Fung Wah* porn, its primary focus is on the blowing.

And so it was an operative of the Chinese government's Ministry of State Secrets found himself putting the Pleasant Valley Sunday Rehabilitation and Psychiatric Treatment Center in Camarillo under electronic surveillance. If Fung Wah had realized at the time the direction that request for his help would have taken all of them, he never would have placed that call. But his lack of foresight is to be forgiven. After all, the only person any of them knew of with the gift of prescience was unavailable for consultation. She was hiding, apparently from them, with a bunch of crazy people and alcoholics in Pleasant Valley.

Fung Wah could think of far worse valleys a person could be hiding in. American politicians and their famous friends on the TV news like to talk a lot about a valley of the shadow of death and the evils that lurk there. He was greatly relieved the Wu had not gone there to hide. Not because he didn't think she could handle it, but because he didn't think his nephews could. Especially Pat Robertson.

CHAPTER TEN

Dr. Carlson was not at all happy with the way things had gone in his evaluation of the clinic's newest patient. As much as he struggled to stay on track, Morgan La Fay seemed to have a gift for getting him to talk about himself. On more than one occasion he impatiently insisted they stay on topic, but the patient merely pointed out each time that they were already on a topic and it was a perfectly suitable one.

"Doctor, you seem reluctant to explore your fear of demonic possession."

She spoke in such a disarmingly soothing voice that he relaxed his professional guard and began telling her about a disturbing incident from his childhood. He and his sister were actually confronted by a demon that almost pulled her through the bedroom wall while hissing through crackling flames that it was claiming her immortal soul.

"Doesn't it bother you that your belief in demonic possession directly conflicts with your scientific training from medical school, Doctor?"

He just sat and blinked. It wasn't often he found himself at a loss for words. Especially with a woman.

"Because if you were to take into consideration what you've learned as a scientist, it might warrant further examination of the incident and help you put it to rest. When is the last time you discussed that event with your sister to get clarification on the accuracy of your memory?"

The line of questioning was deeply unsettling. His sister had long since debunked the entire incident as nothing more than fanciful imaginings brought on by seeing the Disney animated movie, Peter Pan. But Ben Carlson knew better than to believe his sister, whose memory of the incident couldn't possibly be any more accurate than his. She was, after all, only a female.

"I would like to discuss these voices that you claim to be hearing, Morgan. What are they telling you?" He was certain he had successfully changed the subject and steered it away from himself, at least for the time being.

"What can one say about periodically hearing the voice of reason, doctor? Like any voice in the back of one's head, it sits there quietly until one is about to make a boneheaded move and then indicates it has an alternative move to suggest by first clearing its throat loudly to get your attention."

"And when is the last time this voice of reason

spoke to you, Ms. La Fay?"

"When I was on my way here to Pleasant Valley Sunday with that killjoy."

"And just why do you consider coming here to be a boneheaded move?" He was beginning to think he may actually be getting somewhere with the patient. "Does it make you uncomfortable to be around people with problems similar to yours?"

"Doctor, you keep trying to make this about me when clearly it's about you." There wasn't a hint of the exasperation in her voice her words might otherwise have implied. Even though he pointed out firmly he had chosen a profession which involved working with others such as herself in need of psychiatric care, a profession for which he had trained for years, she managed yet again to change the subject and bring it back to him.

"I cannot imagine a single institute of higher learning that teaches students of psychiatry that mental illness can be attributed to demonic possession, doctor. You are a man of science yet it seems you have yet to embrace the science enough to objectively examine your superstitions, which are clearly at odds with it."

"I'd rather keep the focus on you, Morgan. Let's discuss your mirror-touch synaesthesia, shall we?"

"My what?"

"What I am told you call being an empath is in fact a rare neurological condition."

141

He explained that neuroscientists regard the condition as a state of "heightened empathic ability." He said they think the condition is an extreme form of a basic human trait, to which Constance Void replied it was just the opposite: not having the ability to feel what others feel is an extreme form of a basic human trait. And not a desirable one, either.

"And what basic human trait would that be?"

"Psychopathy, Doctor. Duh."

"Your condition is the reason you don't leave the house much and don't own a television, isn't it?"

For a brief moment Constance was stumped. She honestly didn't think Suzanne Shill had been listening to her when she told her about the last time she watched television. It was a program where a man killed a sweet little rabbit he intended to eat for dinner. The Void felt as if she had killed the rabbit herself. For days. She put the television out on the curb with a sign that said, "GRATIS," and was relieved when it disappeared. Within minutes. We are talking about Oxnard, after all.

It was also the reason she didn't eat any animal products of any kind. She could feel the animal's suffering as she ate. It was nauseating. And it made her realize there really was no difference between human slavery and animal slavery, but knew better than to bring that up, having heard all about the doctor's religious peculiarities. She knew exactly where any discussion about slavery with him would end up. The last thing she needed was to get embroiled in an argument about the intersection of slavery and sexism with a black religious fundamentalist who chooses to embrace a belief system that includes headship.

"Zann Killjoy tells me you can also pick up on what people are thinking with real accuracy. That's the stuff great spies are made of. It could have made you a good candidate for the intelligence industry. The CIA, for instance. They could have put you to good use. Did you ever consider that?"

The Void shrugged. It was nothing like when Atlas shrugged. In fact it was more like when Diogenes shrugged. She told him she did think about it but two things kept her from applying. She was absolutely certain the moment they found out about what she was capable of they would dissect her brain. He had to admit she had a point, the CIA being what it is.

"The other reason?"

"Torturing people would be more pain than I could endure. And we all know how much the CIA loves to torture people. They don't do it because it gets reliable results, you know. Torture never does. They do it because they like doing it. One of the perks of the job, I guess. Weren't we just talking about psychopathy? I couldn't be in the same room with people like that. The black hole of their souls would suck me right in. Is it true no light escapes those things? Besides, they would never be willing to let me get the information my way."

"Your way?"

"As you said, I pick up on people's thoughts with uncanny accuracy. What fun would that be for the CIA? They would never stand for it, perks being perks and all."

"So basically you're saying your synaesthesia is the reason you don't work. Right?"

"Wrong. Agoraphobia."

"You're about as agoraphobic as I am a Swiss masseuse."

Constance Void groaned and told him she preferred they didn't discuss massage. And of course Dr. Carlson insisted they discuss it. She explained she made a little extra pocket change by giving friends and neighbors massages. He failed to see why that would be a subject she wouldn't want to discuss. Perhaps there was something salacious she preferred to keep to herself? Ben Carlson was not about to let it go. But she did warn him, didn't she?

"How does giving others massages affect your synaesthesia?"

"Pleasure, Mister Twenty Questions. Aside from getting a little extra spending money, I get a massage given to me by myself through the feelings of the person I'm massaging. And damn I'm good, even if I do say so myself. Hell, it's the only way I could ever get a

144

massage, since I can't afford to pay for them at those fancy spas with all their scented candles and lotions."

"What about the men in your life? Don't they ever give you massages?"

Constance Void was almost bored with the question. Any woman will tell you a man only gives a woman a massage as a seduction technique.

"Why do men only touch a woman as a prelude to sex, Doctor?"

Ben Carlson didn't understand the question. Why else would a man touch a woman?

"Speaking of sex, there's something I've always wanted to know about mirror-touch synaesthesia." A grin involuntarily crept across his face. Constance could already see where this was going and didn't like it. Not one bit.

"What does it feel like when you watch pornography?"

"Why don't you go fuck yourself and then you'll know exactly how it feels. Pervert."

It was at that point Ben Carlson knew any attempt to gain control of the session was a losing proposition. The devil was in his new patient far too deep. He was even more sure now of the message he'd found from God earlier. When he opened the patient notes he kept in a Word file, there was a thumbs up emoji next to the brief notes he'd made based on his meeting with Zann Killjoy. It indicated the clinic's newest patient was the perfect candidate for psychosurgery.

He busied himself with her chart notes and dismissed her without another word. As she walked from his office he pictured her sitting with all the others in the activities room braiding lanyards and friendship bracelets for the Boys and Girls Club annual fundraiser, not a thought in her head. If the Lord hadn't wanted Ben Carlson to use his skills to make the willful woman submit to the subservience He had chosen for her when He created woman out of Adam's rib, he wouldn't have given him the skills, would he?

For the past few years Ben Carlson had been privileged to what he believed was a most uncommon dialogue with God. It started shortly before he had begun doing his now trademark psychosurgery. He had only just begun exploring the idea of it, researching the history of surgeries on the mentally afflicted, looking specifically for a way to permanently disrupt any connection in the brain between what those Hindu freaks called the Third Eye and the Crown Chakras. He was certain it was the source of demonic possession and only attracted the attention of Satan and his minions. Otherwise, why would those Hindus draw a red bullseye right in the center of their forehead?

He had been having some success with a chemical disruption of that connection, but knew patients were still at risk, especially those who were prone to discontinuing their medications. More and more he found himself thinking about the surgery. He would see it in his dreams, and felt the hand of God turn his attention in the direction of surgery at unexpected times, such as when he would be inexplicably inspired to turn on the television just as a science program exploring brain surgery was airing. Or a random ad for a movie about some brain eating psychopathic cannibal would flash the image of an exposed brain on a billboard during his commute to the clinic.

What stood out for him about both of those random events was he never watched the science channel, and only kept the television tuned to the 700 Club. Nor was he accustomed to turning on the television that early in the day. The 700 Club only aired its women speakers at that time of day, and hearing what women have to say about God disinterested him for obvious reasons.

And the thing with the billboard was even more intriguing because just the previous morning a new ad had been put up on that same billboard which showed a scantily clad Victoria's Secret model. He said a prayer for its removal. Out loud. Interestingly, other motorists were saying a similar prayer that morning, but it was for the removal of what the model was scantily clad in. But not the wings. She can keep the wings on. Please.

After some thought and discussion with his accountant he decided there was ample room at the clinic for a well-equipped surgery, and plenty of profits from cutting corners in the cafeteria that needed to be reinvested anyway. There were more than enough funds to finance the necessary upgrades. It was a relatively simple procedure. All he needed was the perfect candidate, and he trusted God would guide him in that direction when he was ready for it.

And so it was God's delivery of his first chakra severing psychosurgery patient happened right there at his desk. Before leaving work each night he would make notes on the patients he'd seen that day with such things as his impressions, concerns, and whether a patient needed an increase in medications or another one added to what he'd already prescribed. He would enter these notes into the computer he had in his office, but because of their highly sensitive nature, as well as confidentiality laws, they weren't accessible to anyone but him. They were, in fact, heavily password protected, even from the other staff. As well, his computer was neither connected to the clinic's computers nor to the internet. The last thing he needed were prying eyes questioning his methods.

One night he finished the last of his notes by entering one in the form of a question. Nothing surprised him more than to find the very next morning his question had been answered. Of course, the question had been whether a certain patient needed psychosurgery or not. And what he found when he opened the file the next day was a thumbs up emoji next to the question, indicating the answer was yes.

Upon some careful examination, Ben Carlson confirmed his computer's operating system didn't even have the capability of making a thumbs up emoji. Who else could it have been but God? It was the kind of conclusion any rational man of science would have come to in his position.

The patient had begun hearing voices shortly after giving birth to her first child. Anti-psychotic medications had helped to control the voices, but some well-meaning counselor had advised her to take up meditation and yoga, and even though the patient insisted her ensuing psychotic break had nothing to do with that, Dr. Carlson knew better. The patient felt the precipitating factors in her break were the death of a parent, loss of her job and subsequent foreclosure of her home. But Ben Carlson wisely pointed out that had she not opened the door to the devil, those losses wouldn't have occurred in the first place.

The surgery was a success. Not only did the patient stop hearing voices, she became more docile, passive and grounded in her femininity. Noting all of it in his Word file, it didn't surprise him to find a thumbs up emoji at the end of his summary the very next day.

It took a while for him to get the hang of the somewhat awkward, cumbersome system of communicating with the Omniscient, largely because he kept forgetting to put his questions in a simple yes or no format. But when he did, there would invariably be an answer waiting for him the very next day, each and every time. At first he questioned whether God would need to use a computer to communicate with him. Or with anyone, for that matter. He remained skeptical until he began noticing something else. Ben Carlson's dreams on those nights he had left a question were always about doing surgery on that specific patient, and he saw it as having as much significance as the thumbs up emojis.

There were times when he had left a question asking God whether he should tell others about the help he was getting from Him. But each time he posed the question it was met with a thumbs down emoji after a night of dreams that were clearly reminding him God works in mysterious ways. In the end, he decided it honored God to say nothing and trust the Divine Mystery, and to do that he needed to keep his uncommon dialogue with the Omniscient to himself.

The psychiatrist knew researchers had discovered mirror-touch synesthetes tend to have a greater volume of gray matter in areas of the brain linked to social cognition and empathy, and less brain volume in the temporoparietal junction, which plays a key role in distinguishing self from other. So that's what he decided he'd target in his surgery on Morgan La Fay. He would tell the insurance company it was to correct a debilitating Depersonalization Disorder.

The surgery would be almost identical to all the other surgeries he'd done. And this one would feel especially satisfying. The reason was simple. God did not intend for us to be connected to other people, empathically or otherwise; only to Him. Carl Jung and his devotees could go to hell with all that new age collective consciousness bullshit. There was only one powerful mind that mattered, and it was the Omniscient.

Which was why Dr. Carlson only kept the television tuned to Flocks News in the day room and did not allow any kind of popular music to be listened to by patients or staff at the center. The only culture anyone needs is the culture of worship. The only story a person needs to read or write is the story of our Lord. The only song a person needs to sing is the song that gives full attention to the Lord.

All this nonsense about coming together and giving peace a chance is the work of the devil. It's the devil who wants to see us give our full attention to each other and focus on the human condition because it means we've turned our attention away from God. God needs our full undivided attention at all times.

If Constance Void had been in the room she would have read those thoughts and asked the only logical question to ask:

Why is God so needy? Does he have low self-esteem?

And knowing the Void, she probably would have continued on that train of thought and posed another question:

If God had low self-esteem it would mean he didn't have any faith in Himself, which would make Him an atheist, wouldn't it?

As he was entering his notes in the file about the session he'd just had with Morgan La Fay, including those about the surgery he would be doing on Sunday, the irritating woman suddenly reappeared in the doorway.

"One more thought; in the form of a question."

Ben Carlson considered dismissing her, but was curious to know what her question was. Considering God never seemed to mind the questions Ben had for Him, he felt it was only right to pass along that favor. He nodded for her to continue.

"How would you even know whether it's the devil speaking to you, or God?"

He was about to launch into an explanation of the inherent fallibility in those who are untrained and therefore unprepared to know the difference, especially women, but she held up her hand.

"Don't answer that, doctor. It's a rhetorical question. One that something told me you needed to hear." She seemed to be turning to leave, but another thought crossed her mind.

"And as long as you're giving that some thought, you may as well toss this one in: Since the voice of God must pass through each man's personal filters, which are entirely based on that man's life experiences, how can we ever know something hasn't been lost in translation when the man claiming to have information given to him from God then passes that information on to the rest of us?"

He wanted to answer her. Truly he did. But he couldn't get past the discomfort he felt having her read his mind, and it was making him lose patience with the woman. He didn't think Morgan La Fay could tell how angry she'd made him because of how well he'd learned to hide his feelings. Until he remembered she not only knew the feelings of others, but felt them as well. Which meant she was even better at hiding her feelings than he was.

He wanted to ask her why she hadn't gone into medicine herself, used her ungodly curse as a diagnostic tool, until he remembered when he'd had to do his surgical residency. There was no way she could perform surgery on anyone. The patient wouldn't feel a thing because he would be under anesthesia, but the surgeon had to stay conscious. If that surgeon was Morgan La Fay she couldn't possibly endure that kind of pain. The thought made him shudder and it surprised him. The idea of the demonically possessed eliciting feelings of empathy in him made him even angrier than he had been.

When the door opened again moments later, he jumped from his chair and shouted, storming toward it, angrily assuming it was her again.

"Look. A man knows exactly what God is telling him only if he has accepted Jesus Christ as his personal Lord and Savior. Then and only then will he truly know the infallible voice of God. Until then, any voice a man hears in his head is the voice of the devil or one of Satan's minions. And since women are incapable of having a direct relationship with God, it can only mean when they're hearing voices in their head it's Satan. Plain and simple. Got it, Ms. La Fay?"

He was unable to see past his own boiling temper until he was across the room and standing face-to-face with Haj, not Morgan La Fay. Haj had endured the voices in his head long enough. He'd simply had it, and was stopping by because he wanted to know more about the doctor's miracle surgery.

Ben Carlson's rant only confirmed what he'd suspected all along, even if he was a Muslim man. The Jinn didn't care. The Jinn wanted his soul and that's what it was going to take if Dr. Carlson didn't agree to cut that part of his brain out soon. And as far as Haj was concerned, it couldn't be soon enough.

CHAPTER ELEVEN

Somewhere in Temple City a young Italian bride is
stirring freshly chopped kale into a steaming pot of
wedding soup and asking herself why it always comes
out so gassy. Perhaps if she had heard of the legendary
gaseousness of the infamous *Fung Wah Soup* she
wouldn't have been so concerned about how her own
soup might affect her in-laws visiting from Verona.
    While little explanation can be given for the
gassy nature of wedding soup, it's clearly obvious that
the good uncle's soup is made that way from using
wakame and kombu in the broth. The mineral rich sea
vegetables impart a delightfully complex flavor, a
flavor some may even describe as playful. But
unfortunately along with that flavor comes the

invariable price. The young bride from Verona could be consoling herself right now with the knowledge that things could be worse; she could be serving her already long-winded father in-law the windiest soup on the planet.

If there's anything other than breaking wind that relieves the disquieting tension which builds up from too much pressure, it's perspective. And it was perspective Agent Toole was hoping for when he stopped by the Shanghai Noodle Factory on his way back to his cubicle. Just three doors down from the Fung Wah Herb Shop, the Noodle Factory's egg flower soup was legendary throughout the city. That being said, had Toole known he might have been able to sample something more playfully complex than egg flower soup, he might have been tempted to stop in and give the ancient herbalist's broth a try.

But the NSA analyst's senses were off and he suspected it was due to the excess sugar from all the pudding he'd been eating. He needed brain food, and nothing said brain food more than a raw scrambled egg poured into a pot of boiling chicken soup.

Toole needed to focus now more than ever. There was too much at stake not to be at the top of his game. He had managed to stay on Admiral Thomas Thumbsen's tail after leaving La Salle High School despite the unforgiving afternoon traffic.

From Pasadena the admiral took a route back

into Los Angeles that was becoming all too familiar to Toole. It came as no surprise to him in fact when he saw he had come full circle as he watched Thumbsen enter the Israeli Consulate.

The midget who had led him to the men in robes who then led him to the admiral from Ventura County and the explosive plot he'd diffused just hours earlier had led him finally to Mossad.

The only thing missing was the Chinese, and as he opened the carton of steaming egg flower soup, he told himself that would have to do for now. The office was quiet that late in the evening and it gave him time to take a few deep breaths and think. He'd had a close call back in Pasadena and it rattled him.

It all started when he decided to stay for the reception being generously hosted by the Christian Brothers in the school cafeteria. It was not the kind of choice Toole would ordinarily have made, due largely to his proximity to breathing people making words come out of their mouths in a crowded space. But the admiral and his driver had accompanied two of the Brothers and it became apparent to Toole the alumnus had a fondness for both men in robes. He couldn't help but wonder how much of it had to do with those robes.

He was trying to blend in with the crowd of milling breathing people, straining to overhear the words coming out of Admiral Thumbsen's mouth, when he noticed his driver drift away from the admiral's side, which seemed curious to Toole because it left the senior officer defenseless.

The driver then joined up with a group of graduates in uniforms. Toole counted eight of them in all. All wore the Navy JROTC insignia except for the admiral's driver, who seemed to be secretly leading them to an early grave.

Toole watched the operative nod his head in the direction of the adjoining kitchen and the young men eagerly grin after seeing the staff had left it empty. Toole watched in horror as the driver maneuvered the young cadets into an enclosed space which had no exit except back into the cafeteria.

With nothing between the kitchen and dining area but the serving counter, it was as if they were in a fish bowl. Even the admiral seemed to notice, locking eyes with the driver briefly before smiling grimly and shaking his head.

When Toole saw Thumbsen shrug his shoulders, he knew it could only mean one of two things: either he was in on it, or he was clueless to the coup about to go down. With all of the Navy cadets cornered like that in the kitchen, a single attack could wipe out all of them in a matter of seconds.

Was it all part of a plan to eliminate anyone who might know about the admiral's connection to Mossad? Had those bright young minds he spoke so highly of in his commencement address begun to suspect what

Toole knew about the alliance? Had they begun to pose too much of a threat? His mind raced as he scanned the room for signs of the impending attack. Would it be a bomb? Automatic weapons? Or perhaps just a simple grenade was all that was needed, considering the close quarters the targets were in?

And then he saw them: The midgets. Dressed in white and carrying serving trays, their backs were conveniently turned away from Toole and he was certain it was deliberate. They knew if they showed their faces it would betray the deviousness of their murderous plot. Everyone knows midgets can't hide their emotions. They always carry their hearts on their sleeves.

Without a moment to spare, Toole rushed for the kitchen. Yanking open the door, the words stuck in his throat as he tried to alert the young men of the danger they were in.

Wide eyed, hands trembling, for the first time Toole realized the kind of danger this mission had thrown him directly in the path of.

Still unable to speak, he propped the door open with one foot and held up his NSA credentials, motioning for them to disperse. And it was none too soon. As the young men scurried out of danger, they left a trail of smoke behind them. It could only mean one thing: the bomb was already in the room. And it had been lit. The skunk-like odor of the burning fuse was unmistakable.

Agent Toole had to think fast. And he was certain that fast thinking saved lives, even if by setting off the fire alarm it resulted in the sprinkler system being activated and several people being injured when they slipped on the wet polished linoleum. Toole never could understand why women wore shoes like that to potentially dangerous events like this.

By the time they had evacuated the building and he caught up with the midgets wearing white, he could see they had been cleverly replaced with very short freshmen. And because their young faces showed no emotion, he knew the next generation was already being groomed to take the place of those who had just graduated. When Toole noticed the admiral's driver pointing him out to Thumbsen, it occurred to him for the first time flashing his NSA credentials might have tipped his hand. But it had been worth it, hadn't it? Besides, he hadn't given them his name.

Using his peripheral vision the best he could while appearing to be checking the watch he wasn't wearing by holding his wrist up toward the sky, he spotted security cameras on either end of the parking lot and realized it didn't matter. If they didn't already know his name, they would soon. It was time to get back to the office and place orders for some electronic intercepts of his own.

But first, he fully intended to follow Admiral

Thomas Thumbsen and see to whom the traitor was reporting.

But after less than an hour Thumbsen and his driver emerged from the Israeli Consulate and headed for their car. And curiously, the man in the red yarmulke he'd seen in Venice was with them. It was too much of a coincidence to be a coincidence. And when he saw where the three men were headed after following them, Toole was absolutely certain it was no coincidental coincidence. He watched them go into the Performing Arts Center, where the evening performance of *Fiddler on the Roof* was about to begin.

He knew he could wait for the performance to finish and continue to follow them when they came out, but he was getting pretty hungry, having eaten nothing all day but chocolate pudding. Plus, Toole suspected he would get far more information from putting the admiral under a comprehensive electronic surveillance. He would even be able to track where Admiral Thumbsen's car was through its on-board navigation system.

Thinking he'd have the entire office to himself the rest of the night, he'd planned to start the ball rolling on that electronic surveillance, knowing getting one authorized for the Israeli Consulate was going to be much trickier than putting one on Thumbsen and his driver. He was just beginning to contemplate putting the Performing Arts Center under surveillance when his thoughts were abruptly interrupted by his supervisor's unexpected arrival.

"Agent Toole, I need to see you in my office. Now."

Toole thought it odd his supervisor would insist on the privacy of his office when nobody else was there. But then again, the framed commendation signed by the Secretary of Defense he was certain he was being given was probably on his supervisor's desk. After all, Toole hadn't been there all day, so what else would the supervisor have done with it?

He tried to feel bad that the poor man had to return so late in the evening to finally present him with the award, but considering the admirable job Toole had done thwarting that bombing in Pasadena, he just couldn't muster a single bad feeling. He'd earned the commendation and he knew it.

The man gestured for him to take a seat across from his alarmingly oversized desk. "Toole, we all know the only reason you're working here is your mother. She was the agency's top data analyst, and it was a shame we had to lose her the way we did. But we've tried to honor her memory by making sure you had a place here. Not just so you could follow in her footsteps, but so we could keep an eye on you."

Toole wasn't sure where this was going, but

bringing up his mother couldn't be a good sign. After twenty five years of distinguished service, the respected NSA analyst had fallen prey to a perplexing psychiatric condition that has been known to befall others in the field: *Apophenia, or false pattern recognition.* It proved to be devastating for his mother, and tragically, deadly.

Toole's mother had become absolutely certain she had found a connection between the 2009 coup in Honduras, the popular conspiracy theory about the Israeli's illegal organ trafficking being tied to Big Pharma, Mossad's mind control technology, and the other popular conspiracy theory about man-made nude beaches in cities being built deep underground in mountains around the world by the corporate elite, who apparently knew something the other ninety-nine percent did not.

It all started when she was assigned the task of decrypting some data recovered from an intercepted device that was found on the roof of a house across from the Brazilian Embassy in Honduras after the coup. Everything about the device pointed to the Israelis, including the words *Made in Israel* stamped on it.

It was obvious to Toole's mother what the device was for, having worked closely with the Defense Department's own equipment designed to intercept all electromagnetic transmissions coming into and going out of the embassy.

When used correctly, incoming transmissions can be altered to say anything. It had obviously been placed there in order to induce confusion and panic in the few people that had not fled the embassy. The entire thing was pretty uninteresting to her, until she decrypted the data that was stored on the device. It was about the Israeli cooperation with the Chinese.

What she found connected the massive profit both the Israelis and the Chinese are making in illegal organ trafficking and generic pharmaceuticals to the cost of building their latest city, deep inside Cerro las Minas, with pristine nude beaches where the corporate elite can run around in their bare feet without getting covered in tar balls.

She could easily see what an attraction it would be for any wealthy CEO to go to a beach that hasn't been spoiled by any oil spills. And since there's nothing but artificial light that deep inside a mountain, nobody has to worry about getting sunburned. Hence the *nude* part of the *nude beach* feature.

Toole's mother jumped to her death from a passenger jet twenty minutes outside of San Pedro wearing nothing but moisturizer, dark sunglasses and what she thought was a parachute but in fact was the backpack belonging to a kid from Amsterdam who had been staying at youth hostels while hitchhiking across

America before crossing into Mexico and making his way to Central America.

Had she bothered to open the backpack before jumping, she might have seen he was financing his trip with a large supply of organic TrainWreck from Humboldt County. The young pot tourist found it much easier to sell it at airports than at truck stops, but didn't have much luck selling it in either Mexico or Central America. They have enough of their own.

Of course, Toole never believed for one moment his mother could ever have made such an amateur mistake. It just wasn't in her nature to miss something so essential to her survival. This was a woman who would tell him from ten yards away he had a button loose on his shirt. And you better believe she knew whether he'd put one coat of polish or two on his shoes.

"Let me just get to the point, Toole. I got a call from Admiral Thomas Thumbsen today asking if the NSA had him under surveillance. He said you'd been at a graduation in Pasadena and for some reason were involved in setting off a fire alarm that resulted in several people being injured when the automatic sprinkler system was activated.

And then after that you tailed him to the Israeli Consulate where he's consulting with them on reaching an amicable solution to the blockade of Israeli ships by protesters in the Port of Los Angeles.

After that, you followed him and an Israeli diplomat to the Performing Arts Center. I wasn't sure I believed him until I got ahold of the surveillance footage from the parking lot outside that high school and saw you standing there looking up at the sky like you were looking for bunny shaped clouds. I honestly couldn't believe you would do something like this."

He could see he'd caught Toole off guard. Leaning across the desk for emphasis, he locked eyes with the agent and frowned.

"Did you really flash your NSA credentials to a bunch of kids smoking pot in the kitchen, Agent Toole?"

Pot? Suddenly so much made sense to Toole. All of the cadets had been in on it. Why else would they have been burning drugs to mask the smell of the fuse? But how much to tell his supervisor, especially before he had the whole picture filled in? There were pieces to the puzzle that were still missing, and he needed to get that surveillance up and running ASAP.

Toole swallowed hard and prepared to do something he was almost as uncomfortable with as being around real breathing people: he was going to lie.

"It was my cousin's kid, sir. He was graduating and I received an invitation to attend. I was so moved by the admiral's commencement address I wanted to get him to sign my invitation. I would have asked him in the cafeteria, but I smelled smoke and noticed a group of kids doing drugs in the kitchen. I thought flashing my badge would scare them straight, sir."

"And the fire alarm?"

"I have no memory of pulling the fire alarm, sir. I just assumed it was the smoke from their drugs that automatically set off the sprinkler system and triggered the alarm."

The supervisor wasn't convinced, especially considering the young analyst had continued to follow him after leaving the embassy. He'd seen this exact behavior in Toole's mother, and knew to be concerned. Leaning back in his chair, he asked the agent to explain, tapping his fingers impatiently on the desk.

"I followed him from there still hoping to get his autograph. I thought he might go into some public place where I could approach him, but when he went into the consulate I realized I couldn't set foot in the building, since all I had on me was my NSA credentials. They would have tossed me out on my ear and then notified the media. And the media would have turned it into an international incident."

"That doesn't explain why you followed him after he left the consulate, Toole."

Toole shrugged. "I would have gone into the Performing Arts Center after him, but I didn't have money for a ticket."

He considered changing the subject to the dismal

pay a data analyst makes in the NSA, considering how expensive even simple forms of entertainment are, not to mention the cost of a decent pair of shoes. But he decided to wait until he'd cracked the case and had something to show for his efforts.

The supervisor sat staring at him for several awkward moments before sighing and shrugging his shoulders. He had no reason to accept the agent's story, but he also had no reason not to. The analyst had a clean track record, and except for his genetics, had never given the agency cause for concern.

After a lengthy lecture in which Toole was reminded the NSA does not have field agents, the supervisor seemed to give in to his own end-of-the-week fatigue. He sternly warned Toole that if it was discovered he was out in the field chasing conspiracies down rabbit holes, he would be suspended until undergoing a thorough psychological evaluation. But for now, the supervisor was letting him go with just the warning.

"I let you take the lead on this alliance you stumbled upon, but you need to do what you do best: analyze data. With your clearance, you should be able to collect enough of that to keep you busy at your desk until you're ready to give me a full report."

Toole's heart sank as he returned to his desk knowing there was no chance he'd ever get clearance to put the Israeli Consulate under surveillance. And he'd drawn far too much attention to Admiral Thumbsen to risk putting him under surveillance now. His supervisor had bought his story, but if he learned Toole had then started collecting the admiral's data he doubted any cover story he came up with to explain would be believed.

Which left him with just one lead to follow: Constance Void. It was time to focus on putting the Pleasant Valley Sunday Rehabilitation and Psychiatric Treatment Center in Camarillo under surveillance. The sooner he learned more about the Void, the sooner he would crack this case wide open. And the sooner he would know what he needed to about those midgets. And the Chinese, hopefully. Because at this point, the only thing he knew about them for sure is they make a fine bowl of egg flower soup.

CHAPTER TWELVE

Fung Wah's contacts in the Chinese government seemed especially jovial when he asked them about putting the treatment center in Camarillo under surveillance. They were more than delighted to help. It had been a good week for the hackers. They had managed to break into one of the most secure databases on the planet and steal information on millions of American intelligence personnel. While the politicians' friends and mouthpieces on the TV news speculated endlessly about what they were going to do with the data, Fung Wah was fairly certain the hackers were mostly interested in the health of their organs and so were checking to see if they had selected a PPO or an HMO for their medical provider. Everyone knows belonging to an HMO spells nothing but doom for the health of one's organs. And not just the kidneys. All of them.

Assuming Fung Wah knew what he meant by it, the hacker his contacts once again connected him with asked if he wanted the standard surveillance or the advanced. He thought about the question carefully as he considered the meaning of the word *standard* as compared to the word *advanced*.

The old man's mind wandered briefly to his favorite selection of word porn before giving his answer. Because he would spare nothing in ensuring his nephews were able to safely bring the Wu, he finally and most confidently told the hacker he wanted the advanced surveillance.

The American name which hacker Peter Kim had chosen for himself was Blade, which made no sense to anyone since Peter is already a common name for American men. But Blade thought the name Peter made it sound like he should be running around jumping off of things in brightly colored tights and it made him nervous. He needed to blend in. The last thing he wanted when he came to America was to be mistaken for some American comic book superhero or a character in a Disney movie.

The first time the herbalist asked for his help locating the two women he sought it had taken Blade only minutes to hack into the computer at the Pleasant

Valley Sunday Rehabilitation and Psychiatric
Treatment Center in Camarillo. The process had been
made laughably easy by the clinic's use of a Windows
operating system, since Windows has that handy
backdoor key written into it. Anyone with access to the
internet and a modicum of hacking skills can waltz in
the backdoor of most computers in operation and make
themselves at home, even those used by otherwise
rational professionals intelligent enough to get through
college.

A favorite pastime of Blade and his hacker friends
was to watch bored members of the American
intelligence community, both private and public,
change the results of laboratory tests for shits and
giggles. Then they'd watch notations being made in
those patients' files by clueless doctors and other staff
members about those patients' reactions to the false
results. Nothing was more entertaining to them than
reading notes made about a patient's reaction to finding
out they were pregnant or using illicit drugs. Or both;
especially when neither was possible.

Or what about watching them get cut off from a
medication because their urine test showed they aren't
taking any of it so it must mean they're selling what's
being prescribed to them on the street? Watching them
then go into withdrawals because the careless doctor
hadn't verified his facts before heartlessly believing the

data over the patient was hilarious.

What made it even more entertaining to Blade and his friends was the fact that in America even C students get to practice medicine. Since most members of the US intelligence community were themselves C students they missed the joke entirely.

Of course, more entertaining than any of it was watching those members of the American intelligence industry start up a betting pool between them to see whose predicted outcome would prevail. Would the patient turn to some kind of street drug, or go to an emergency room to beg for more medication? Would he end up getting labeled a "drug seeker" in the medical system and be cut off of all treatment for his condition? Or would he try to suck it up and go through withdrawals on his own? If he did, would he stroke out from seizures or have a heart attack? If so, how much damage would he be left with?

Blade was never quite sure who got more kicks out of all of it, members of the CIA or the private security workers they contracted with. He sometimes wondered if any of them knew he and his hacker friends would amuse themselves for hours watching all of them meddle with people's medical files just for the fun of it.

For Blade, returning to that same system in Camarillo took even less time since he knew the way there, electronically speaking. Getting into the clinic director's computer took a little doing since it wasn't online, but when had that ever stopped him from getting into a computer remotely? If it had the capacity to go online it had the capacity to be hacked remotely even if it wasn't connected.

And finding and opening his password protected private files was just as easy. What wasn't as easy was figuring out what they meant. It seemed to Blade the doctor was having some kind of conversation with someone else accessing the file remotely from another system, and he could see traces of that mysterious someone else's electronic footprint embedded in redundant files on the director's hard drive.

Blade was intrigued. The more he studied the doctor's files, the more he could see that very same someone else in question was directing the psychiatric neurosurgeon to intellectually neuter certain targeted patients by performing brain surgery on them. And he appeared to believe that someone he was having the conversation with was God. At least, that was what it looked like to Blade.

It also appeared one of the patients he was currently targeting was one of the women Fung Wah was looking for. Blade had a feeling his discovery could lead him to a special batch of the herbalist's extra strength aphrodisiac. It could also possibly lead to an increase in status at the Ministry, depending on who was manipulating the surgeon. Maybe even an increase in pay.

The hacker needed to know more. There were security cameras in most of the rooms at the center, but they didn't have microphones so weren't of much help. Blade needed both eyes and ears at the clinic.

He was pleased he'd gotten the go-ahead from Fung Wah for the advanced surveillance because that's what he needed in order to have them. He could see from the surveillance cameras that every employee there was carrying a cell phone. He could also see they were bored with their jobs, because most of them stood or sat with their faces glued to their smartphone screens while the patients wandered around too overmedicated to realize how bored they were. Drooling down the front of their hospital robes really didn't look that entertaining.

Blade had never really seen the appeal of Instagram, Twitter, Facebook or any of those other popular websites. Online social networking in general was nothing more than both the lazy law enforcement officer and the unimaginative intelligence analyst's wet dream come true. Why would Blade want to do their work for them? It would be like jerking off a total stranger and the thought made him shudder. His birth name may be Peter, but he wasn't that kind of Peter.

Tights turned him off.

Even though the public was told the American government had nothing to do with the design and implementation of the most highly trafficked websites, he had looked at their code enough to recognize the handiwork of more than one software engineer receiving a government paycheck. At least the Chinese government didn't pretend they weren't paying their hackers.

Blade knew he could expend the energy collecting the cell phone data the old fashioned way: driving to the clinic with his Stingray and setting it up to collect all the outgoing data. But why bother with something designed for unimaginative American law enforcement officers, who are too busy getting free Starbucks coffee and pastries to do any real detective work?

Designed to mimic a cell phone tower, the toaster-sized Stingray lures all cell phones within a certain radius into connecting to it. Then it's only a matter of collecting all the data those cell phones send out. Not just conversations, but text messages and any browser activity get caught up in the digital gold rush.

Blade considered it a gold rush because lazy American law enforcement personnel were far more likely to blackmail someone with the data they collected than they were to arrest an actual criminal. Unless of course you count the bonuses they receive for meeting their arrest quota, which is more like embezzling, so still fits the profile of basic American corruption in authority.

Of course, what Blade and his buddies enjoyed most about the Stingray was how the device drained the batteries of all the cell phones that connect to it. Listening to buyers of brand new six hundred dollar smart phones complain to their providers that the batteries were defective was hilarious, especially when the customer service representative was as clueless about the Stingray as the customer.

But in the end Blade knew it would be far easier and involve far less driving to simply hack into that room in San Francisco where all American cell phone activity, including conversations, is routed and stored for when some politician needs to be blackmailed.

He chuckled to himself thinking about the many panicked discussions between members of Congress and certain faceless strangers in the weeks leading up to the vote that granted retroactive immunity to the telecommunication companies for collecting and storing all of America's cell phone activity. The FISA Bill made Blade and his Chinese hacker friends happier than anyone really knew.

With the stroke of a few keys, he had gotten more information than he actually needed. It included the names of each bored employee, which then allowed him to hack into their service provider's records. He then used what he found to access their smartphone microphones, including Dr. Carlson's.

Setting up the same advanced surveillance for Suzanne Shill and Constance Void wasn't going to be quite as easy, since the Void didn't have a cell phone and had thrown Suzanne Shill's out the window of the car the night before while running from absolutely nobody whatsoever.

If only the two women had realized two things before racing off in the night like that: the men pursuing them were neither organ traffickers nor computer hackers, and Asians can't drive. Blade would be the first to tell you that. It was his least favorite activity. Getting on the Hollywood Freeway terrified him. He'd rather wear tights. The women could have gone into Krispy Creme, had doughnuts and coffee and gone home in the time it took the brothers from Wu Mountain to get out of the parking lot.

But Blade was confident he would be able to work around the fact that neither woman had a cell phone microphone on her. It would take a little more effort on his part to listen to any conversations each one had within earshot of a cell phone since arriving at the rehabilitation and psychiatric treatment center, but it was definitely doable.

For as long as anyone can remember, people had been claiming to have invented things that the Chinese had in fact been the ones to first come up with. Take the printing press, for instance. Or pasta. The Italians just can't get over themselves, can they? It was no different with hacking telephone microphones and the United States.

While the Americans like to think they developed the technology and first put it to use in the nineties, it was in fact the Chinese. And it was much earlier than that. With the invention of the cordless phone with its battery it didn't take their technicians long to figure out the microphone can't be turned off ever and works as the perfect transmitter. The only way to stop it from transmitting is to remove the battery, which pretty much cancels out its usefulness as a cordless phone, doesn't it?

The beauty of using first cordless phones and then later cell phones for gathering information was it didn't require the cumbersome and often complicated job of breaking into a person's home, office or car to plant a listening device. All it took was accessing the feed remotely. And now with cars coming equipped with programs like OnStar mobile phone voice and data communication systems, it was possible to have a complete surveillance of most people round-the-clock.

While the discovery of this was exciting news for the Chinese government for obvious reasons, it was even more exciting when industrial spies got ahold of the idea. Hacking into a person's phone can be as easy as hacking into any operating system, as long as it's a system the hacker is familiar with. Not only did it revolutionize direct marketing overnight, it changed the nature of economic espionage in ways nobody could have imagined. Blade never did understand why the Five Eyes didn't call themselves the Five Ears.

Because of the Camarillo clinic doctor's status in the community and his income level it was relatively easy for Blade to find ample information on the psychiatrist in more than one corporate database. But what intrigued him most was finding it on one of the private defense industry databases which specializes in serving both commercial and public interests. It was almost too easy a hack, to be honest, and the kind of thing any amateur sleuth looking for a good story to get wrapped up in would find as highly entertaining as Blade did.

What wasn't easy was figuring out who was behind the specific programming currently being done on Dr. Carlson. It was clear that an advanced surveillance had been set up on him decades earlier, because of the telltale deletion of the data from that time, with a vaguely familiar digital footprint left behind. And all the signs were there he was currently being manipulated remotely by someone. But who? And why were so many Americans superstitious to the point of being gullible?

Listening to a recent conversation from the doctor's cell phone feed as he described a supernatural event involving a dream from what he assumed was God about a specific college chemistry exam he had expected to fail, it was clear even at a young age he had no business going into a field that required the study of science. Any kind of science. And it didn't surprise Blade one bit that Carlson was about to flunk chemistry prior to that curiously timed dream. Why wasn't he going into the priesthood? Isn't that what most men who really don't think much of women do?

From the telltale snippets of code left behind when earlier data on him was deleted, it was clear to Blade he was being watched closely by somebody. Perhaps it was someone who might have some future plan they hoped he would be suitable for; maybe someone with a vested interest. But what wasn't clear was who is running the program now. He could only assume it was the same party. The identifying information was obscured in a way Blade had never seen before. He could see it was there, but couldn't trace its origin.

Data on the two women was proving harder to locate. Their names weren't coming up in any files associated with any targeted individuals of interest to the American government, so he checked the corporate databases. Still nothing on Constance Void, but there was enough on Suzanne Shill to learn more about her than he really wanted to. It made him shudder to think how effortless it was to access her complete electronic record and read about what had been learned from collecting her metadata.

The corporate mind game that had been played on her by using that data was pretty cut and dry. Suzanne Shill's programming was exclusively commercial and seemed to involve little more than compelling her to purchase clothing, upholstery fabric and matching accessories in loud obnoxious floral patterns. She was also compelled to buy into a curious American belief system called headship, which apparently stemmed from religious fundamentalism.

Blade wondered if the reason she was concealing her true identity actually had nothing at all to do with hiding from what she thought were illegal organ traffickers. Maybe she was actually hiding from her husband and his handler, a ruthlessly wealthy televangelist named Pat Robertson.

Then he remembered one of Fung Wah's nephews was named Pat Robertson and decided the next time he spoke with the herbalist to ask him if his nephew would kindly give him some pointers on how to get women to willingly be his servant and sex slave. The evangelist made it look so easy on his television program to convince women they are nothing more than the byproduct of man's superfluous appendage, but so far Blade had not had any luck making one believe she was inferior to him and therefore owed him sex whenever he demanded it. Without reciprocating any kind of pleasure whatsoever in return. He had tried telling women giving him pleasure should be all the pleasure they need, but it never worked. They always just left angrily and blocked his phone number.

The televangelist's reasoning for his curious focus on the man's pleasure only was ingenious. He had apparently programmed his subjects to believe women were only supposed to focus on the man's pleasure because it was sinful for women to experience any kind of pleasure for themselves other than the moral reward that came from satisfying their man. He couldn't wait to meet Pat Robertson and shake his hand.

Finding anything at all on Constance Void was impossibly frustrating for Blade. Not only was there no cell phone or internet data on her, like what he'd easily found on the wallpapered woman, he couldn't locate her on any database under any name. Not even by running her photo from the Krispy Kreme parking lot through Interpol's facial recognition software. It was as if she didn't exist.

Blade wondered if perhaps she had also been programmed to buy into the evangelism. Do American women who are subjected to the evangelism become so convinced of their own inferiority to men they begin to fade until they become transparent and their data so faint that it disappears altogether? Is that what happened to Constance Void? But that made no sense at all.

For one thing, there was nothing in the news about millions of women disappearing after being enslaved by the evangelical programming and gradually becoming transparent. And for another thing, the very fact that her face was in the photo captured by the Krispy Kreme security camera was evidence enough that Constance Void was clearly not transparent.

And what was that she was throwing at Pat Robertson's feet, a firecracker? He was surprised it wasn't something more lethal. It made perfect sense to Blade that any woman would throw explosives at the man who had convinced an entire segment of the population just because slavery had been abolished it didn't mean it had to end. Not as long as there were women around to convince otherwise.

For the time being, until he could get a handle on locating Constance Void's data, Blade was going to have to rely on the feed from the various cast of characters at the Pleasant Valley Sunday Rehabilitation and Psychiatric Treatment Center run by a psychiatric neurosurgeon who seemed to be convinced he was performing surgical brain mutilations in the name of God. Including the wallpaper obsessed woman who had been a subject of the Pat Robertson programming to willingly be the slave of men just like Dr. Carlson.

Every time Blade saw American politicians on television making religious statements while on the campaign trail they always seemed to be echoing the fundamentalist evangelical sentiment. And there was always a good woman standing behind each and every one of them, much the way feudal lords did with their servants in the Dark Ages.

Any hacker could easily confirm the politicians in America are owned by the same people who own the media, which means despite what they like to tell themselves, America really does have a state sponsored religion. After all, doesn't their currency say *In God We Trust?* And don't all the cameras focus on what church the political candidates belong to at election time?

Blade found himself wishing China had a state sponsored religion like America does. He could use a good woman to stand behind him and serve him. A women who would bring in some extra income and do all his cooking and cleaning, especially the woodwork, which needed a woman's touch.

He was, after all, no Peter Pan in tights. The hacker couldn't remember the last time a woman had polished his wood. Blade would very much like to be

calling out God's name while a woman did that for
him, even if he was an atheist.

CHAPTER THIRTEEN

"Let's get settled in so we can welcome our newest visitor to Pleasant Valley Sunday."

The latecomers were still scurrying into the room. As they slid into their chairs the group therapist checked her Twitter feed one last time before silencing the smart phone for the hour.

"But before we do, I have some announcements. First, Dr. Carlson will be performing back to back surgeries day after tomorrow, and since there are so few staff members on duty over the weekend, those staff who are here may be busy assisting him. He asks that patients try to do their very best without a lot of staff attention.

And speaking of Dr. Carlson, some of the staff have noticed Glenn Greenworld standing in the hall across from the doctor's office pointing at his door. Glenn, we need to ask you to stop. It's unsettling to the staff and to Dr. Carlson. Also, it's been reported that you've been doing yoga in the unoccupied rooms late at night, and as I know you've been told more than a few times, the clinic strictly forbids doing yoga."

Not being one to sit on a question, Constance Void raised her hand. It felt vaguely like being back in grade school, and considering both the institutional plastic chairs they were sitting on and the tone of voice the group leader was using, it was understandable.

"Why is yoga forbidden here? I mean, I can understand the thing with T'ai Chi, but how is yoga a problem?"

The woman looked around the room and sighed before answering.

"Since you're new here and this is your first group therapy session, I will let it slide that you have spoken out of turn, Morgan. As for yoga, we must respect the religious beliefs of the majority, and the majority here believes yoga is nothing more than a doorway through which Satan or any one of a number of demons can enter the soul."

Constance wanted nothing more than to explore the therapist's delusion by asking for a vote to see if the majority of the group agreed with this notion, but the therapist continued as though the matter was settled.

"The same goes for meditation, in case you weren't told during your orientation."

Constance thought it curious that two of the things proven to be most beneficial for recovering addicts and for many mental patients as well were forbidden at the clinic for reasons related to religious superstition. She told herself to ask Jerry if he could do a search of stockholders in pharmaceutical companies and see how many of them had ties to fundamentalist religious leaders. Somebody had to be profiting from these ridiculous notions, and it sure as hell wasn't the patients.

"This is her first group session with us, so let's introduce ourselves to Morgan La Fay." She was addressing the group in a voice that sounded like they were kindergärtners.

Constance waited for the woman to introduce herself first, but she didn't. *Did this mean she doesn't have a name? Surely she has to have a name.* But for the life of her Constance could not find out what it was. Even later when she asked around. Nobody seemed to know. She glanced around the room at the looks on the faces of everyone sitting in those plastic grade school chairs and was pretty sure they were all faking it, hoping she would eventually introduce herself. Apparently she never bothered to. Ever.

One by one, the patients said who they were and gave a brief explanation for why they were at the clinic. Some Constance already knew from her adventures in the halls and day room the night before, or from the cafeteria at breakfast and lunch. She was so touched by the stark honesty so many of them showed It stirred an honesty in her that made her glad Suzanne wasn't there. The Void opened up and spoke more truth about herself than she had promised her court appointed therapist she would.

"My therapist – Zann, whom some of you have met, thinks I'm suffering from some kind of psychosis where I think I'm something I'm not and hear voices that aren't there. She thinks this *delusional system* compels me to do and say things that get me into trouble. But everything I do and everything I say is for a perfectly good reason, and the trouble I've gotten myself into has been a necessary part of carrying out what it is that needs to be done."

"So you're telling the group that you acknowledge getting into trouble, but it was trouble that you intended to get into?" Constance nodded her head and started thinking of possible names for the therapist.

Prudence?

"So what is it you think you are doing?"

Wilomena?

"Reversing the curse, of course. It's truly the only thing that can be done with shenanigans."

It was a simple, straightforward answer she assumed anyone would understand, and from the many nods coming from around the room, Constance saw most there did. Except for the trained professional, who only scowled and tried to look authoritative.

Gertrude?

"Morgan, surely there must be some part of you that knows what you just said doesn't make sense." But before Constance could answer, another patient interrupted.

"It makes perfect sense to me." Jerry had interrupted without raising his hand. It made Constance imagine he was pretty good at holding his own in the arguments that break out in the comments on YouTube videos.

"She is named after a sorceress, after all. It only stands to reason Morgan La Fay would be qualified to undo whatever harmful magic has been done in the world."

The trained professional attempted to take back control of the group but it was too late. A discussion erupted that she was unable to contain, much like the comments section on YouTube videos, but of course in real life. Except for Jerry. Everybody knows Jerry lives on the internet. And for him it is real life.

Their discussion was about the nature of the evils that surround all of us, who might be profiting from it, and who would most likely be qualified to help balance the imbalance of power that has grown so out of control in the world.

"I don't like to refer to myself as a sorceress. It sounds entirely too old-fashioned."

Jack Kerouac was intrigued. He liked watching definitions of words grow and change more than anything, being a strong believer in cultural evolution. And while he would never say so in mixed company, he secretly admired John Yoo for the enviable job he'd done of redefining the meaning of the word *torture*.

He honestly couldn't believe UC Berkeley had hired Yoo on as a professor of law after completing his tenure in the Office of Legal Counsel for the Bush administration. It was clearly obvious the man was a truly gifted fiction writer and should have been considered for teaching creative writing.

And who could forget the remarkable job the Mormons have done of completely obfuscating the meaning of the word *soliciting?*

Before he could let his thoughts wander too far off topic, Jack asked Constance what she prefers to call herself. After a few moments of awkward silence, Constance Void, née Morgan La Fay, gave the group her answer.

"I like to think of myself as an Absurdist Voodoo Priestess. Largely because nothing disturbs evil more than being laughed at, and because most of my incantations involve large amounts of pudding.

Chocolate pudding. And midgets, of course. With toilet paper."

"Midgets with toilet paper?" It didn't surprise Constance Void that the only anthropologist in the room would be asking for clarification on that. She looked at Carlos and shook her head.

"No, the incantations have toilet paper. The midgets like to carry sharp objects."

The therapist who had lost control of the group put her head in her hands. She knew better than anyone in the group magic doesn't exist. And even if it did, it had no place in a rehabilitation and psychiatric treatment center. She began muttering under her breath.

"Magic cannot cure madness."

"Did I just hear you say magic cannot cure madness?" Haj sounded terrified.

The therapist was aghast that she had actually muttered those words loud enough to be overheard. It is never a good idea for any trained mental health professional to refer to mental illness as madness. That would be crazy. She sat like a deer caught in headlights, except her huge dark eyes failed to reflect anything because she just couldn't see the light.

"She is wrong, is she not, Miss La Fay?" Haj's voice had become shaky. He turned to Constance, who sat next to him. She heard the pleading in his voice clearly and it broke her heart because there is nothing more heartbreaking than the silent noble suffering of a dignified man being driven mad with shenanigans. Especially the kind of shenanigans Constance had sensed were at play here at Pleasant Valley Sunday. She'd been feeling it since the moment she stepped through the front door. She gently nodded her head and smiled warmly.

"Yes, Haj. She is wrong. Mostly. Ordinarily, magic cannot cure madness, unless of course the madness was brought on by magic and its evil twin, the Lord of Shenanigans."

She reached for his hand and gently squeezed it and he did not recoil from the touch of a woman to whom he was not married. To him, it was the loving touch of his mother telling him her love endures and so will he.

It was Carlos who broke the spell the patients seemed to be under when he suddenly spat out an accusation. "This is bullshit. You do not have one single shred of evidence that you have these magical voodoo powers. It's as if you're deliberately trying to be different from the rest of us. I bet you haven't done a single spell in your life."

The group members began to grumble and the therapist tried in vain to quiet them. But it was Glenn Greenworld who succeeded in getting everyone to use their inside voices when she asked Constance to give them an example of a spell she'd done using pudding that had been successful.

"It came to me in a dream. And it involved a leaf blower, toilet paper, two mop handles, some duct tape and chocolate pudding in a cup. I was guided to a GWEN tower in south Oxnard at the edge of a field of strawberries.

The words for the incantation just came to me as I was reciting it while unloading eight rolls of toilet paper and two packs of chocolate pudding in a cup directly onto the tower in a matter of seconds. It was at that moment I knew I had found my voice. And with my voice, I had found my power as an Absurdist Voodoo Priestess."

"Did it work?" Jack Kerouac wasn't the only patient on the edge of his seat dying to know how it turned out. But as a story teller, it was understandable to Constance that he was eager to see where the story was going. Constance Void nodded.

"How do you think we got Edward Snowden's revelations?"

She shrugged her shoulders modestly and tried hard not to absorb the skepticism that was oozing from Carlos.

The therapist rolled her eyes as the room erupted in applause. All except Carlos, who rolled his eyes, as well. Nothing he'd just heard made any sense at all. Why would a person go out of their way to be so different it was absurd?

He had a sense that day's group therapy was

pretty much over, and so did the therapist. Making a note to speak with Dr. Carlson about the infectious nature of the new patient, she dismissed the group and reminded everyone of the curfew.

Constance couldn't see that there had really been anything therapeutic about the group, and wondered if the whole point of it was actually just to get everyone there used to hearing what mental patients talk about, since they would most likely be members of that club for the rest of their lives. Why not get used to each other as soon as possible? This is America, after all, the place where being stigmatized for receiving mental health care is a national pastime.

She would tell you to just ask Bill O'Reilly, but he was busy on the screen in the day room shouting at people about the importance of taking the vote away from mental patients and didn't want to be interrupted.

"Our night staff reports some of you were up prowling the hallways late last night again. So I need to remind you all patients are restricted to your rooms after ten PM. That means you don't belong in the day room."

Constance thought the therapist sounded particularly winded as she made that last announcement and wondered why. Had she been doing her kegal exercises as she sat there in her little plastic chair, just so she'd feel like she got something worthwhile done? Doing those things can become an addiction if you're not careful. Then it hit her.

Jane. Her name is Jane.

As she headed for the cafeteria to see what that awful smell was, Jerry ran to catch up with her. He'd been slowed down by the lag on his connection while trying to do a search on GWEN towers and was curious to know why she'd picked that as the target for her incantation. After all, the Ground-Wave Emergency Network was nothing more than a communications system that the military constructed in the nineties to provide an alternate means of communication in the event that something were to disrupt those that rely on signals higher up in our atmosphere.

GWEN operates at a very low frequency that tends to hug the ground. Since such low frequencies drop off sharply with distance, the towers were installed to be from 200 to 250 miles apart, making a total of about 300 of the eyesores stretching from coast to coast across the US.

He was dying to know why she would target one, and whether it had anything to do with the fact that since the towers are now stationed coast to coast they're bathing the entire civilian population with ELF waves.

"I have no idea. It's what the dreams told me to do, and I never disobey orders that come from my dreams. After all, we've all got to serve somebody.

But the results were only partial.

Whistleblowers are still being prosecuted now more savagely than under any other administration. I think it may need to be redone with more than just me there working the magic. The bigger the effort, the bigger the results, right?"

The Void seemed to interrupt herself as she changed the topic without warning.

"But that's hardly the issue now, is it, Jerry?"

She had stopped abruptly and turned to face him, lowering her voice to almost a whisper as she searched his eyes. "What do you think is slowing down our wireless connection here? Because dude, it's driving me crazy, and this is definitely not the kind of place one should be in when one finds oneself going crazy."

Relieved that he was not the only person there to have experienced the lag, he smiled despite the seriousness of the subject. It was that involuntary smile that sneaks up and attacks at the most inappropriate of times, that ridiculous unintentional and entirely uncontrollable grin at a funeral or when passing a gruesome scene along the highway. Jerry had tried to do a search on it but had been largely unsuccessful at finding an explanation for the phenomenon that made any sense to him.

"I thought it was just me! I ran that defrag this morning and it didn't help. It's like there's some kind of interference in the connection itself here at Pleasant Valley Sunday. Do you think there could be some kind of third party intercept on the line?"

Constance had only her instinct to go by when she nodded. Yes, it was most likely some kind of intercept, possibly routing them to the kind of connection that nobody wants to be exposed to. Not only was Jerry at risk of picking up a virus, but he could end up having some nasty spyware installed on his hard drive through the backdoor key. Or worse, malware. Malware can make an operating system do things nobody in their right mind would ordinarily do. Or even most crazy people, for that matter.

"The only thing I know of that will protect us is to boost our gamma wave activity. They oscillate at different frequencies and are harder for a third party to intercept and tamper with. In fact, it's impossible to install spyware or malware when there's a lot of gamma wave activity."

"How do I do that?" He was truly regretting he couldn't do a thorough search on the subject of brain waves right then and there, but he did quickly bookmark the Wikipedia page so he could go back and absorb the information later.

"Basically, you have to open the door to the devil." She was grinning mischievously.

"You mean meditate?" Constance nodded and winked.

Neither of them realized Carlos was right behind them, listening. He had been shadowing them, craning to hear what he could of the conversation since leaving the group, having taken it upon himself to police the whole *Opening the Door to Satan* threat. At the point that he heard Morgan La Fay suggest to Jerry he meditate, Carlos began to scream and went running for the nurse's station.

"I am genuinely worried about Carlos. Any idea how we can find out his last name so I can send out some smoke signals and see if we can get the poor dear some help?"

Despite the clumsiness and obvious drawbacks to the antiquated analog communication system, Constance Void was relieved smoke signals were still working flawlessly. As flawlessly as can be expected, at least. Steganography is not an exact science and is often up to interpretation. But at least it can't be decrypted, even if it is intercepted.

"Castaneda. I did a little digging when he first got here and I needed to look up the word xenophobia. Did you know Flocks News is the first definition that comes up on my search engine?"

"Seriously?"

"Absolutely. Check for yourself. Flocks News is synonymous with xenophobia."

"No duh. You know very well that's not what I meant. I meant Carlos. His name is really Carlos Castaneda? That's a rather ironic name for an anthropologist who's a xenophobic pantheist, isn't it?"

Jerry nodded as they reached the cafeteria and Constance saw what the awful smell was all about. In institutions like Pleasant Valley Sunday they like to call it *dinner.* It smelled even worse than lunch had, and Constance Void hadn't thought anything could smell worse than that, which is why she skipped it. Now she was hungry and considering offering to drink Jerry's can of Boost for him. But then she remembered all the sugar in it and was pretty sure she didn't want to end up with the runs.

At the end of the serving line stood a modest salad bar with a bowl of sodium benzoate soaked chunks of iceberg lettuce and several smaller bowls of shredded carrot, red cabbage, sunflower seeds, raw broccoli florets and grated cheese.

Bypassing the bowl of poisoned lettuce, Constance piled the other ingredients except the cheese into a disposable plastic bowl and grabbed some lemon wedges to squeeze over all of it, hoping it would fill her up. Falling asleep with a grumbling tummy was never easy, and her lack of sleep the night before as she got her bearings at Pleasant Valley Sunday left her needing some decent REM sleep.

Nothing was more important to Constance Void than her dreams. They had been her guide, her candle in the dark, the compass that kept true north no matter what since she was a young girl.

Some medium on Ventura Boulevard had told

her many years after the dreams had begun she was a prescient dreamer. The Void was grateful for something to finally call the dreams that would tell her of future events. Some had helped her avoid certain dangerous situations, for which she was eternally grateful. Some would give her a heads up on certain natural or man-made disasters that would then unfold. But for the most part they seemed to only be about telling her to celebrate the random.

Sometime after midnight, Constance Void found herself pondering yet another random thought. She couldn't help but wonder why they called it a day room, considering it always seemed busiest at night, despite the curfew.

The only patients who could be found there during the day were the ones who were so heavily over-medicated they couldn't do anything more than sit in front of the television and drool. She also couldn't help but wonder if exposure to that much Flocks News, especially so heavily medicated, could do real and permanent damage to the psyche. And not just the psyche of the already mentally ill.

Since all psychotropic drugs reduce brainwave activity to a steady, predictable frequency, it seemed to Constance they made it much easier for organizations like Flocks News to program people. She really was pretty sure that's why they called it programming.

In fact, she had to admire how adept the

network had gotten at Neuro Linguistic Programming, since post hypnotic suggestion works best with a medicated target. How curious the staff at Pleasant Valley Sunday had no problem with hypnosis, but forbid meditation. She had to wonder if they'd all gone to the same evangelical university the pundits flashing their identical smiles and haircuts on the television had.

The whole issue was the reason she didn't use drugs of any kind, especially alcohol. Except the TrainWreck, of course. Without it, smoke signals would be impossible. But that goes without saying, doesn't it?

In her experience, drugs tended to make it easier for forces outside her control to manipulate her, and she was adamantly opposed to being manipulated, on general principles. Especially by forces outside her control.

After all, why do you think the Church insisted the Renaissance artists who painted the many variations of the Last Supper all included that chalice of wine in the Messiah's hand right smack in the middle of the painting? As far as Constance Void could see, it was the first example of cultural programming through product placement. It doesn't take a genius to see it's much easier to manipulate a population of drunk people, since their behavior is so much more predictable.

As well, she was certain that her own limited exposure to Flocks News just from walking in and out of the room was the cause of the dream that woke her and sent her wandering the halls in the middle of the night. In it, she was randomly sharing a cup of chocolate pudding with Bill O'Reilly, Dick Cheney and Pat Robertson. And curiously, all three seemed to be surrounded by a mighty wind that blew on and on, with a beautiful dancing boy who had the most unforgettable cheekbones and eyes the color of smoke signals. He seemed to be from all four corners of the planet. She woke disoriented and peered through the dark until realizing the fourth corner wasn't there.

Perhaps that's why she found herself in the day room instead of trying to go back to sleep. When incomprehensible dreams keep interrupting one's train of thought, a day room can come in handy, especially at night when one hopes to locate a little TrainWreck to help get things back on track.

And that's just what she found shortly after sitting down with Jack Kerouac. He may not have been the best dresser, or even any good at picking out a pen name, but the man knew his TrainWreck.

Although Constance truly just wanted to sit alone out in the courtyard and try to find an answer about the wireless connection problem by sending out some smoke signals, she could feel Jack Kerouac had something on his mind that was troubling him. She blamed herself, since it was her tale of midgets and chocolate pudding that had disrupted the group therapy and kept him from bringing it up there.

"I know you think I'm just another alcoholic writer," he said bluntly, which Constance found ironic since they were sharing a blunt. "But it didn't start out that way. I've been given some information that needs to be carefully handled, and the burden weighs on me."

She honestly couldn't see how that was any different from all the other writers out there who weren't drunks so worked to find the right words to keep the conversation going. And the blunt.

"Information? Like the information about celebrating the random that's cleverly woven into Forrest Gump? Or more like the information about staying away from eating liver at family dinners that's written into Portnoy's Complaint?"

Jack Kerouac shook his head to both. He really did seem to be burdened with something, so she did her best to help him feel he could share more than just the blunt with her. It had burned down to almost roach-clip length before he finally told Constance what was at the heart of it. His best friend had been employed with a private security firm in Orange County, where most creepy people go to live and work in Southern California.

Constance wondered briefly if the creepy guy

she'd been sitting next to at the Ventura County
Courthouse lived in Orange County, which of course
led her to wonder if he'd gotten that document to Roz
she asked him to. So much of her plan hinged on the
bailiff getting that information. But Jack Kerouac
pulled her attention back to the dying blunt roach
between his fingers and the story he was telling her.

Graham had been a data technician most valued
for his skills as an archivist. He'd been assigned the
arduous task of cleaning up a massive quantity of files
being transferred from one server to another for the
CIA.

He was mostly bored by the repetition involved
and not really paying a whole lot of attention to the
content of the files until one in particular caught his
attention. Unlike the others which were labeled
"Classified," this file was labeled "Top Secret." It was
titled "Operation Mockingbird." He'd heard stories
about the existence of it, but always thought it was just
another conspiracy theory. But here was the file. He
couldn't help himself; he had to read it.

The first section of the file dated all the way back
to the 1950s and outlined a plan for influencing the
media, including television, film, print and radio.
Having heard rumors about the CIA's involvement in
popular culture, he was curious to see just what their
objective was. It turned out to be nothing short of

enslaving the minds of the American people.

Once he got past the outline, page after page of reports spanning decades detailing one operative or another's infiltration of a television studio, newsroom, writer's group or movie production team left Graham certain he had just pulled back the curtain on Oz. He was seeing something he could never un-see.

Mockingbird included not just popular media, but public education and of course religious organizations, specifically fundamentalism and its handmaiden, televangelism. Of course, the IRS has cooperated fully with the CIA in ensuring televangelism flourishes, exempt from being taxed on the billions the ruthless industry rakes in annually. And for which the central banking system is eternally grateful.

Unlike the corporate elite, televangelists spend cash like a crack whore on a binge. After all, somebody's got to circulate cash so economist's figures show a robust economy.

Over the decades, there was no organic element of the American culture left. None of it had grown out of the common experience of the people. All of it was carefully orchestrated, manipulated and produced with the expertise of the finest director in Hollywood.

Even though Operation Mockingbird was disbanded in the 1970s as a result of the Church Committee's investigations, it went underground and slithered back out with a new name and new purpose.

Project Chaos wasn't content with merely enslaving the minds of the American people; it needed to ensure the public suffered total blanket amnesia. History forgotten is history repeated for profit. And what the CIA was doing was all about profit, just not for the American people.

The best way to induce that amnesia was with drugs and chaos; the kind of drugs that are addictive and the kind of chaos that spreads contagiously with a handy little plot device called terror. Reducing America to nothing but factions was much easier to do when pointing the finger of blame at factions from far away with a different skin color.

"Graham realized too late he would have been better off not paying attention to the file. There were hundreds more pages of reports he just had to finish reading. But he knew if he took more time than necessary to clean and move the file it would raise suspicion, especially a top secret file. So he copied it to a flash drive and took it home with him. It didn't take long for him to realize that had been a big mistake."

Constance Void closed her eyes and saw exactly where he was going with the story.

"Let me guess. He gave it to you with instructions to go public with it if anything happened to him. And then something did happen to him."

Jack Kerouac didn't respond and it was all the

answer she needed. She'd heard about the nasty games the children play with each other when they get into fights over their childish games, and wanted nothing more than for all of them to grow the fuck up before they blew up the planet. But of course she didn't say that. She said nothing because she knew he wasn't done talking.

"They took control of Graham's car remotely and crashed him into a tree going 120 miles per hour on a residential street in L.A. I wasn't one bit surprised because the night before he saw it in a dream. It rattled him so much he called me at four in the morning to meet him. Told me about the dream, the top secret information that clearly showed our own government working to enslave the minds of the American people, and about the copy he'd made of it.

Then he told me something so cryptic that only he and I would get the reference. I knew instantly that's where I would find the flash drive. When they killed him, I went and got it. It was exactly where he said."

It was the classic story. If Constance had heard it once she'd heard it a hundred times. But she wasn't quite sure where it was leading. Why didn't his friend use the dream sensibly and avoid the situation he was being warned about? Did Jack Kerouac learn the obvious lesson and go out and buy an old Rambler instead of continuing to drive a computer with wheels which is easily hacked? And of course, the most obvious question: why would the information drive him to drink?

It wasn't until he explained he was a fiction writer that she understood. He'd had a couple of modestly successful books of fiction published, and if he tried to write a non-fiction exposé based on the material he now had, it would get buried on the internet with all the other conspiracy theories by the many conspiracy theorists claiming to have the exposé of the century. And the information was far too important for something like that to happen to it.

"So what's your point? Fact is always stranger than fiction. People are invariably more likely to believe fiction over the real deal. Why do you think we have the term *Suspension of Disbelief?* For that matter, why do you think we have a never ending election cycle?"

"So what are you saying?"

"I'm saying you should write it as fiction. If anyone comes after you, just tell them you pulled the whole thing out of your ass. At least you will have gotten the story out there."

She could tell from the silence and Cheshire cat grin it wasn't something he'd thought of. And obviously nobody had advised him to consider. She told him to make it the bestseller he'd always dreamed of writing. That way, it would hit the widest audience possible, and the information would be impossible to take back or bury.

While she appreciated the stimulation of both the conversation and the TrainWreck, Constance Void needed to find a way to relax. Since she'd been asked to not do T'ai Chi, she excused herself and went in search of a quiet spot to do a little yoga. Maybe she might get lucky and find Glenn Greenworld and she'd point out a good place to do it. She was absolutely certain that anyone at risk of being demonically possessed as a result of being in close proximity to someone doing yoga was already in bed asleep.

Grateful for the Chuck Taylors that allowed her to noiselessly prowl the halls, she wandered through the deserted night in a futile search for that elusive spot in the medicated quiet of sleeping Pleasant Valley mental patients. Until she came around full circle and found herself back in the day room. The over-medicated droolers were gone. The catatonic bipolar with Tardive Dyskinesia from too much lithium who spent his days rocking in his chair had been led back to his room to rock himself to sleep. The addicts and alcoholics had been given a pat on the back for making it through another day.

What was left was a woman whose superpower is pointing, a xenophobic pantheist, a kind faced Muslim desperate to escape the wrathful magic of the merciless

Jinn, and a no longer alcoholic writer who had recently resolved to find a pen name better suited to him than Jack Kerouac.

In light of news he'd recently heard from Jerry about the confusion over Kerouac's actual cause of death, it just didn't seem right to use that name any more. Why tempt fate? The last thing he needed was to leave behind any more conspiracy theories for people to bloviate about on the internet.

All were seated facing the television as Jerry, who claimed to have just downloaded and burned a copy of the latest remake of the Manchurian Candidate, loaded the disc into the day room DVD player. Constance liked that the real threat, the menacing entity behind it all, had changed from the Red Menace in the original to American politicians and their corporate handlers in the remake. It seemed more realistic to her. The whole Red Menace thing had been a red herring the whole time anyway. It was about time somebody got with the program and started calling out those corporate shenanigans.

Once back in her room, Constance Void was well on her way to having the best night's sleep a person in a mental institution has the right to. And it began with the noticeable absence of dreams about Pat Robertson, Dick Cheney or Bill O'Reilly. She did however have a dream about Roz Ferriday and a

Rastafarian from Venice Beach. Things went downhill from there. A person knows they've hit rock bottom when they dream about midgets and pudding for the third night in a row.

CHAPTER FOURTEEN

After accessing the data streams on both Psychiatric
Neurosurgeon Dr. Ben Carlson and court appointed
therapist Suzanne Shill, LMFT, who was apparently
using the unlikely name of Zann Killjoy as an alias,
Toole turned his attention to Constance Void. But when
he returned to his desk with a fresh cup of pudding and
some leftover battery acid from the staff coffee pot in
the break room, he was surprised to find nothing
pertaining to the Void had downloaded from the
mainframe.

From the conversations he was able to access
between Suzanne and the doctor, it was clear the
therapist had admitted Constance to the clinic. He
chuckled to himself that she'd been admitted under the

name Morgan La Fay.

That's our Void. Never misses the chance to show off her expert training.

But absolutely nothing came up on any database indicating the *steganographer* had ever existed. It was as if she had lived her life surrounded by a Faraday screen and no electromagnetics had been able to get in or out. Was that why she'd been recruited to do the work she does so well? Was it really a coincidence she was passing coded messages on to an officer of the court whose last name happened to be Ferriday?

As far as he could see, she'd never owned a computer, never used one at the library, did not own a phone of any kind and except for the grainy photo from the Krispy Kreme parking lot, there were no photographs of her. Had she never had a driver's license because the camera couldn't capture her face? Perhaps Toole had discovered an entirely new species. Or an anomaly: the Girl in the Faraday Bubble.

If so, it was no accident the surveillance camera got a photo of her. She let it happen. But why would she want that one photo to be left behind? Was he expected to believe it was merely an accident? And if she never used the computer at the library, how was she planning on doing online therapy with Suzanne Shill? Come to think of it, hadn't she said it was her snooping on the internet that led her to discovering the alliance of the sixteen badly behaved Jewish midgets?

How exactly was she accessing the internet; invisibly?

He decided to put the whole thing on a back burner to simmer, hoping it may produce a thought that would wrestle him free from the conundrum, and turned to the data collected on Dr. Carlson and Suzanne instead. Their conversation intrigued him. Constance Void showed no signs of being delusional in her behavior when Toole sat next to her in that courtroom. And the document he'd intercepted showed the workings of a perfectly lucid mind. Yet both the court appointed therapist and the psychiatrist were in agreement that the Void couldn't possibly have the insight into midgets that she obviously has; even if she is calling them by a completely inappropriate name.

After listening to the doctor's story about the chemistry final in college, Toole decided to take a closer look at the psychiatric neurosurgeon's data stream from that time. Curiously, the file had been deleted. Since no file can be deleted without the electronic signature of the party who deleted it, Toole went in search of that. What he found instead was what looked like the logo from the bottle of generic Dramamine he kept in his medicine cabinet for those rare occasions when he had to travel. Toole was prone to motion sickness. Unless he was behind the wheel of the car, he had to take the Dramamine.

Why any pharmaceutical company would hack

into the Defense Department's mainframe and delete decades-old data on a medical student was beyond Toole. Until he read the doctor's journal and the personal notes he kept on his patients. Somebody was obviously taking advantage of the fact the psychiatrist was so superstitious. Among other things, they were hacking into his patient notes with smiley faces and thumbs up emojis to make the doctor believe he was being directed by God to perform a radical brain surgery on certain patients. Toole was certain of it. And whoever it was had both the expertise and equipment to get into a computer that wasn't even connected to the internet. That limited the potential suspects to a small field.

Like his mother always said, anyone who believes in coincidence just isn't paying attention.

Oddly, Toole could find no common thread among those patients targeted for the surgery. The random assortment had included a citizen journalist, professor of sociology, high school civics teacher, an animal rights activist who was also a vegan advocate of organic farming, a chemistry researcher, at least one Christian Science atheist who didn't believe in God or doctors, and the few high school graduates who had actually learned critical thinking in Ventura County public schools. And because of the surgery all of them would now be spending their lives unable to do much more than make lanyards and friendship bracelets for the Boys and Girls Club rummage sales.

They would also be taking powerful pharmaceuticals to control the violent seizures left behind by the surgery. It seemed the manufacturers of pharmaceutical drugs were making out like bandits from the deal. It also seemed at least at first glance that somebody considered critical thinking to be a threat. And Christian Science atheists, apparently. But that was just the way Toole was inclined to think, being his mother's son.

Toole's toe had begun to tap nervously on the floor beneath his desk, which only happened when he suspected he was onto something he really didn't like. Where had he seen this before? He knew he'd seen it somewhere, and not too long ago. He got up and paced the length of his cubicle, which wasn't far, so it quickly became more like walking in circles until his head began to spin and he had to sit back down. Spinning, thinking, thinking, spinning, spinning, thinking.....where had he seen this before?

And then it hit him. The last time he'd had a case of the tapping toe circular cubicle pacing spins after discovering something unsettling. It was just after one of those all-too-frequent mass shootings. When one of the gravely wounded survivors turned out to be an advice columnist he was fond of because of how much she reminded him of his mother, he decided to look into the tragedy himself to see what he could find. When he went to examine the data stream of the shooter though, it had been deleted just after the kid was hospitalized for breaking his collar bone skateboarding two years earlier.

When Toole went to see whose electronic signature was on the order to delete the data, he found nothing but a vaguely familiar logo. The data that should have been there for the entire period between the kid's hospital stay and the shooting simply didn't exist. Toole had never seen anything like it.

He had no idea who the curious logo belonged to until on a hunch he decided to look at the data on those who didn't survive the shooting. It took a while before he got to the young blogger who died at the scene. The reason she'd started blogging was nobody would listen to what she had to say about the corporate pharmacy chain she worked for and the corrupt dealings it had going on with the pharmaceutical company belonging to that logo. It was the kind of story that could have done real damage to both parties if it had been taken seriously and gotten picked up by mainstream media. Her last blog entry was about having been contacted by a reporter from the Guardian and the supporting documents she was delivering to him the following week.

The spins Toole had gotten that day came from realizing he'd just connected some dots that could either get him promoted, fired, or killed. And because Toole wasn't sure which, and his mother wasn't around to advise him, he said nothing to anyone about what he'd found. Nobody was more powerful or lethal than the pharmaceutical industry. Throughout the recent Great Recession it was the only industry that continued to show robust growth and mad profits. Globally.

But here he was, sitting and staring at the same logo attached to the file from which Dr. Ben Carlson's data had been deleted. And while he had no proof that it was the pharmaceutical industry behind the doctor's mysterious computer dialogue, all of his instincts told him it was. What was worse, the most recent exchange between *God* and the psychiatrist at Pleasant Valley Sunday had to do with targeting his newest patient, Morgan La Fay. Apparently, the doctor's meeting with her didn't go well.

It was bad enough she challenged his knowledge of the obvious role of demonic possession in mental illness, but the doctor made it clear in his notes he was personally insulted when Constance Void inferred he wouldn't know the difference between the voice of God in his head, or that of the devil.

If Agent Toole was going to get to the bottom of the alliance between Mossad and the Chinese, he needed the Void's brain intact. And judging from the doctor's most recent notes and the emojis left in response to them, he didn't have much time before it no longer was.

The thought occurred to Toole that other than checking for a driver's license he hadn't bothered looking at any of the data on Constance Void prior to her going into hiding in Camarillo. So he did a search on any and all data on her going back three decades, assuming he'd find more information than he could possibly need. But there was nothing. Curiously, there wasn't even a Department of Motor Vehicles record on her as far back as he looked. No bank accounts, no utilities, no credit records of any kind.

It didn't look to him as though it had once been there and then been deleted. It looked more like she hadn't even existed. The thought that perhaps Constance Void really had never existed began to wash over him like a huge dizzying wave and he felt his toe getting the urge to tap.

Grabbing his cell phone, he accessed the photos he took of the document he'd intercepted and as he read it again, the wave receded into the deep from which it came.

Constance Void was definitely a real live breathing person, he was sure of it. He had sat next to her and heard her speak actual words out of her mouth, had felt her breath against his face when she leaned into it and

222

looked in his eyes as she spoke those words.

He had seen the look on Roz's face when he handed her the document the Void asked him to deliver, and that alone should be confirmation the Void actually existed. There simply had to be another answer. It had to be one more plausible than a Faraday Bubble; although the thought of a Faraday Bubble did intrigue him.

And he was fairly certain he found it after he accessed the data stream on the rest of the residents of the Pleasant Valley Sunday Rehabilitation and Psychiatric Treatment Center. In Constance Void's first group therapy session the surveillance camera and group therapist's cell phone picked up both her image and her voice. Toole watched with interest as the therapist warned Constance meditation and yoga aren't allowed at the center because of some kind of religious superstition.

Meditation. He'd heard a theory that a person can become advanced enough in meditation they could actually alter their own brainwaves and disrupt any extremely low frequency electromagnetic waves that might surround them. That had to be it. She had perfected an ability to bend those waves around her.

It didn't explain why there was no data on her stored anywhere, but it could explain why there were no photos of her. And the extreme circumstances with those Chinese gunmen at the Krispy Kreme must have put her in enough fear that she lost the control over her own brainwaves that she'd otherwise mastered. Isn't that why Flocks News works so hard to keep the American people in a constant state of fear twenty-four hours a day?

But Toole also heard her talking about having dreams that prophesied events which invariably happened. Could somebody have been using an advanced algorithm to predict events and then somehow gotten that information to her? Is that where she learned about the smoke signals?

Or perhaps they had been leaving newspapers on her doorstep that had been printed with predictive data. She could have read them not even realizing she was seeing predictive data and the information worked its way into her dreams. If anyone had the skills to do something like that and format the data into an innocuous daily newspaper, it was the Chinese. They had been the ones to invent the printing press, after all.

But why? What did anyone have to gain from it?

Unless their algorithm had predicted something they wanted to hide from someone. Considering how poorly the Chinese stock market was doing, it could very well have been stock tips, couldn't it? What better place to hide data than the brain of someone random who was unlikely to draw attention to themselves? If Toole had thought it through he would have considered the fact that Constance Void did little more than draw attention to herself.

Exhibit A: the smoke signals. Exhibit B: chocolate pudding. And let's not forget the midgets.

The other possibility, though Toole considered it remote, was what physicists had been predicting: while time travel itself would never be possible, it would definitely be possible one day for data to be sent back in time. And we were very close to that day being upon us.

It would mean valuable data being moved back through time would need to be stored somewhere reliable, and there was no guarantee today's ever-evolving storage devices would even be usable by the time that data was ready to be retrieved. The only truly reliable storage device is the human brain.

Did somebody know something about the Void's future actions that made her brain the perfect storage device for data from the future? If so, there were only one or two countries that could be involved. One of them was China.

And then there was the other thing Constance Void said in the group. She told them she had been the one to attack the GWEN tower in south Oxnard. When it first happened, it sent a shock wave through the intelligence community. While some just saw it as a simple case of vandalism or a poorly executed attempt at emulating Banksy, Toole had to wonder if that same someone was trying to send a message to the NSA.

One that said, "I'm on to you. Don't think you can just sit back and eat pudding, because I am going to wipe your ass with this mess I've just made."

Was it a coincidence she'd targeted that tower, considering who controls them? After all, while the top of the GWEN towers are used by the Department of Defense, the base of all of them have long since been leased to corporate interests; and all of those corporate interests are owned by the Chinese and their favorite trade partners: the Israelis. Once again, China was coming up at the top of the short list of suspects.

So why then were the Chinese shooting at Constance Void in the Krispy Kreme parking lot? Once again he found himself wondering if they had really been shooting at her or only making it appear that way. The Chinese are masters of deception. Is it possible they only wanted to make it appear like they were trying to shoot her in order to draw suspicion away from them when she finally disappeared off the radar for good? Hadn't Constance initially thought the gunmen were Chinese illegal organ traffickers?

If the plan was to harvest Constance Void's brain in order to extract the data Toole was certain they had stored in it, there was no time to waste. The doctor was planning to mutilate her brain on Sunday morning. The Chinese connection had been staring him in the face from the Krispy Kreme surveillance video the whole time. And if he knew the Chinese, they would make their move some time before the scheduled surgery.

Toole went back into the employee break room and helped himself to another cup of pudding. He'd put it all together. And it felt damn good. The only missing piece at this point was Mossad. And he could think about them on his way back up to Ventura County, since he knew he wasn't going to get the whole picture without being in the field. Maybe he'd relax and take the commuter train. He could always rent a car when he got up there. But then again, riding the train would mean he'd have to take the Dramamine.

And just like that he got it; the Israeli connection. His Dramamine was generic. So were the drugs being prescribed to Dr. Carlson's patients, and not just the ones on whom he'd performed surgery. All of his current patients were on medications. Most, if not all of them, would be taking those generic drugs for the rest of their lives.

There's nothing more valuable to a pharmaceutical company than a sale that's locked in for the long term. Reliable, predictable revenue that can easily be leveraged against and used to multiply stockholders' profits.

While most American pharmaceutical companies follow a more classic model, routinely *evergreening* their products just as they're about to go generic by reformulating one or two inactive ingredients so they can continue charging top dollar for them, it's the manufacturers of generic drugs who quietly make out like bandits. While *evergreening* draws negative media attention and ongoing scrutiny by regulators, nobody thinks twice about the mad profits in generics that pour in under the radar. And who is the largest manufacturer of generic pharmaceuticals in the world?

Toole typed the question into his search engine and waited for the answer, though he was fairly certain he already knew what it was going to be. The largest manufacturer of generic pharmaceuticals in the world is owned by the Israelis and guess what their logo looks like?

"Fuck Big Pharma and the opium war they rode in on!" he said, shaking his head as he licked the last of the chocolate pudding off his plastic spoon.

CHAPTER FIFTEEN

Fung Wah was certain from the persistent knocking it wasn't something he should ignore. And when he found Blade standing at the door to the herb shop he was even more certain. Not just because it was far too early in the morning for anything that wasn't urgent business, but because of the look of urgency on Blade's face. Had the old man not been preoccupied with tying the sash to his robe, he might have looked more closely. Had he done that, he would have seen something resembling panic in Blade's eyes as well; which was understandable. If that mad scalpel-happy doctor in Camarillo succeeded in his plan to cut into the brain of the woman Blade was supposed to keep an eye on, the herbalist may withhold the aphrodisiac the hacker so desperately needs.

As Blade and his hacker comrades had been unable to master the technique used by the evangelists to get women to be their sex slaves, they were forced to resort to aphrodisiacs as their only option. The old fashioned approach of getting them in the mood by drugging them did still work for hackers, after all.

Although, in America it seemed to be more popular to drug them with things that put them to sleep, or to get them so drunk they passed out. Blade couldn't see the sport in that. Unless of course the point was to avoid the look of disappointment on the woman's face after the man was finished. But thinking about how much he tended to disappoint women wasn't what Blade came there to do. He had urgent information for Fung Wah.

"That doctor who runs the clinic has scheduled an operation on Constance Void for tomorrow, sir. He plans to cut into her brain and sever the connection between her Third Eye and Crown Chakras."

"But tomorrow is Sunday. What kind of doctor schedules surgery on a Sunday?"

"The kind who doesn't want to draw attention to what he's doing, since all of the knowledgeable credentialed staff will be off duty for the weekend."

Blade explained what he'd found out about Dr. Ben Carlson's odd relationship with someone pretending to be the doctor's god.

"Which one?"

"Which what?"

"Which god?"

Fung Wah struggled to think of any god who would want someone to sever a connection that is so essential for the Wu. That link between the Third Eye and the Crown Chakras was vital to her receiving the powerful visions and healing insights the world needs.

Perhaps rather than a god it was one of the Four Fiends, in which case it would have to be the *Hundun*, fiend of chaos. Without access to either the Third Eye or the Crown Chakra, the mind would be nothing but chaos. Fung Wah shuddered at the thought.

"The only god they've got."

Fung Wah half-expected Blade's response. He had always been puzzled that the Americans were so intent on limiting themselves to a single deity. What if it was a fallible deity, or prone to going on hiatus periodically to recharge its deific batteries, as all deities need to do from time to time? What if people grew tired of a jealous, vengeful deity and wanted one unlike a human man, with a little less wrath and a more stable temperament?

If Suzanne Shill had been there she would have attempted to explain the nature of omnipotence to him. But she was not there. Nor was she entirely there where she was needed. If she had been, her client would not be about to have her brain mutilated.

Blade told him whoever was manipulating the doctor by pretending to be God had covered their tracks well because even he had been unable to track them. He also told him from the conversations he was able to observe between Constance and others he had begun to suspect the Void was someone special.

"Special?"

Fung Wah avoided making eye contact with the hacker by pretending to innocently pick lint off his robe. Of course that made Blade suspicious immediately because his robe was polished silk and polished silk doesn't collect lint. He raised one eyebrow and smiled.

"Old man, this woman is more than some squeeze you or one of your nephews is after with that aphrodisiac of yours. And don't try to pretend she isn't. She's not like anyone else I've ever seen. It's like she's protected by some unseen force that either makes her data invisible or prevents it from being collected and stored. I have never encountered anyone with no electronic footprint."

Blade didn't want to tell Fung Wah about the backdoor key, remotely accessing laptop cameras and cell phone microphones, or any of the other trade secrets employed by the Chinese government. Largely because he valued his organs far too much to take that kind of risk.

But he also was reluctant to spill any trade

secrets because China's former domestic security chief had just been sentenced to life in prison for corruption. It was bad enough the man had accepted bribes and abused power, but he also leaked secret documents to a Beijing fortune teller.

What kind of idiot leaks state secrets to a Beijing fortune teller?

Blade was too young to remember Ronald and Nancy Reagan's astrologer, but the Beijing fortune teller wasn't; obviously. Out of an abundance of caution, Blade kept his own counsel about his methods and told the herbalist about what he'd learned of the woman who was calling herself Morgan La Fay.

He told him about her dreams of prophecy, her insights, her ability to feel what others feel and know what they're thinking. He told the old man what he'd learned of her incantations involving pudding and midgets, her smoke signals and her celebration of the random. And he told him about one particular encounter Constance Void had with a patient who hadn't told anyone she was five months pregnant.

"She walked up to the woman and slapped the coffee out of her hand and said her blood pressure was already too high and now the baby was in trouble.

The woman was clearly visible in the footage from the camera, and there was nothing to indicate she was pregnant. But later, a staff member entered into her chart notes the patient had been given a pregnancy

233

test and an examination.

Morgan La Fay had been absolutely right about the pregnancy and the blood pressure. The patient had to be transferred to a hospital and admitted into the ICU for treatment in order to save the baby."

The old man swallowed hard as his thoughts raced to a safe place to hide from telling Blade the truth about the Wu.

"I am absolutely certain if the woman is who I think she is and had access to herbs like yours, Master Herbalist, she would have healed the woman and the unborn baby herself. Which leads me back to you and your three nephews."

Fung Wah could see where this was going. He knew it was useless to profess his ignorance. The hacker had put it all together. Sighing, he waved him over to the counter. Still sighing, but this time with a theatrical exaggeration, the old man casually opened the jar of his aphrodisiac and poured a scoop of it into a small paper pouch. Raising an eyebrow of his own, he shook the pouch in front of Blade's face and smiled.

"Proceed carefully if you don't want this to be the last I give you."

Blade swallowed a silkworm cocoon that had suddenly formed in his throat before continuing.

"The prophecy, Master. That the Wu would come back to us when the signs appeared, beginning with the Three who come down from the mountain to bring the

Wu. They would be bound to the herbs of tradition, and led by a wise elder they would locate the Wu when she was ready to embrace her position on the mountain.

That time would come when she awakened fully to her empathic and healing gifts, her communion with the spirits of the ancestors. She would be known throughout the land for her celebration of the random, her smoke signals and her affinity for little men and their weaknesses, including men in robes. It is their own corruption that she will use to lead them to enlightenment, tricking them with all manner of sweet things, but most of all with chocolate."

Largely because Fung Wah had no way of knowing how much Blade had reported to his employers, he smiled slightly and pressed his hands together as he lowered his head.

"I bow down to you, young hacker. She is indeed the Wu of prophecy, and the Three have been charged with the greatest responsibility of all time. Without the Wu, none of us are destined to survive the darkness that has already cast its shadow over us. Surely you know the rest of the prophecy."

Blade didn't, and he wasn't sure he really cared. It was, after all, part of the ancient mythology of a highly superstitious people, and it meant nothing to him. His was a world of hard science and reason, not superstition; a world of software engineering and hardware rather than one of unreliable dreams of prophecy and meditation for some kind of intangible dubious insight.

After all, when a god speaks to a man, what is said is always subject to interpretation, as all men are fallible. But science is not. A code perfectly constructed in zeros and ones and delivered through a strong connection is something that cannot be misinterpreted.

The good uncle waved Blade back into the modest kitchen and gestured for him to sit while he lifted the tea kettle off the stove top and poured two cups of something herbal that had been steeping. While steam bathed their faces in the beneficial vapors wafting from the cups, Fung Wah explained the rest of the prophecy, which had only been privileged to those who needed to know, for obvious reasons. And as can be expected with the man whose name means *great wind,* he failed to sum up his story in just a few simple words. He blew on and on like the Santa Anas, and while he didn't blow down Blade's house, he did blow away the shutters that had kept him in the dark.

"None of what I say here has been written. It has been passed down through oral tradition only. Powerful words that prophesied there would come a time when the entire world would be gripped by forces so at odds with themselves the collateral damage resulting from their battles would be staggering, and none the least of which would be the planet itself.

Cities would be choked in smoke from their toxic fires. Islands would tremble and mountains would vomit into the air before crumbling. Forests would disappear. The great fish of the sea and antelope of the plains would mysteriously die. Many in the cities would starve to death despite toiling long hours each day to satisfy the insatiable hunger of those corrupting forces in control of everything, including food and water.

Those forces would come disguised as benign and aligned with a great creator, but in fact would be concealing the name of who they really serve.

The more a man was to speak about his kind holy creator the more the awakened ones would know to recognize his face for who he really is and what he was truly aligned with. When it reached the point where those forces took control of the minds and hearts of the people, leaving them all with no true will of their own and almost no ability to see through the veil pulled over their Third Eye, the ancestors would know it was time to waken the Wu.

Those of us who meditate daily are well aware those forces are at work. Even as we speak they are relentlessly banging on the door to our thoughts, trying to get in. They search for us night and day, when we are in prayer and when we sleep. When they succeed –

when they find our weaknesses – they manage to slip through those cracks in our defenses.

When they do, they steal our memories. It is our memories that contain the wisdom that makes us strong enough to stand against them. It is our memories of the prophecy that enable us to know we must be watchful and work together to bring the Wu. And until that time we must pass along the sound and vision, those things that help others to remember and stay the course, to break the hypnotic spell the forces of evil have put so many under. And we must gently encourage others to do the same.

And so it has come to pass the Wu is awakened and must return to the mountain."

"But why the mountain, Master?"

Blade had to admit much of what Fung Wah had just told him mirrored what was going on in the world right then and there. Especially the part that sounded exactly like the corporate dominated world manipulating people and making so many forget.

"What can she possibly do for the people and this planet up on top of some mountain? Isn't she needed among the people she is here to serve?"

"The mountain top is the safest place for her. One cannot fall off a mountain. And it is only from that vantage point that she will be able to clearly see everything that is going on. A thing cannot be healed until the nature of the affliction that wounds it is understood.

But just understanding that affliction is not always enough. It must be studied as carefully as it has studied us. The sleeper who has been put under a spell cannot be awakened until the spell is not just understood, but known. And the first to awaken must take upon himself the responsibility to learn what he must to then wake the others.

No demon has ever been vanquished without first knowing his name. When that happens, no matter what he calls himself, he is powerless to defend himself."

The three nephews had noiselessly slipped into the kitchen completely unnoticed by Blade and the herbalist, which seemed hardly possible considering how tiny the space was. Only Smokey Methson lingered in the little bed he had shared with Pat Robertson. He preferred to continue savoring the smell of the pillow saturated with delicious memories of intertwined limbs and lips which the two young lovers created throughout the night.

It was Bill O'Reilly who finally broke the silence that had fallen over the room when he cleared his throat to speak. Blade was so startled he almost jumped off his chair, which made Fung Wah pleased he hadn't given the hacker something caffeinated.

"The four of us have had that dream again, Uncle; the one with the midgets and pudding."

Four?

Blade counted only three nephews and wasn't sure whether Bill O'Reilly was saying Fung Wah was the fourth. It certainly couldn't have been Blade. The young hacker had been warned by his mother since childhood that he must always be watchful for dreams of midgets and pudding. He was certain he had dreamed about neither the night before.

The only solution to a situation as confusing as this one was to blame it on the caffeine in the tea, but he was fairly certain the tea had no caffeine. So he did what anyone living in Southern California would do in the situation: he blamed it on the Santa Anas.

The only thing that made sense to Blade at this point was to change the subject.

"Ah, Pat Robertson. I have much to ask you about women and how to get them to serve my every need. How do you get them to give you sex without first drugging them with your uncle's aphrodisiac? And once you've had sex with them how do you get them to do it again?"

"I wouldn't know. I only have sex with men."

Blade realized learning Pat Robertson was gay explained a lot of things. Like why he really didn't seem to know much of anything about women. He was beginning to suspect the televangelist was nothing more than an actor on a television show. And not one of those reality shows, either. Everything he thought he'd learned from the broadcasts of the 700 Club was most likely carefully scripted, like any sitcom.

"As long as I live, I will never understand American television."

"But even though I don't have sex with women, there is much I have learned since coming to this country, and I can tell you when a man fails to attend to his partner's needs, stimulating that partner yet not ensuring that it leads to its natural conclusion, he is being rude and disrespectful.

If you are not paying close attention to these women and only thinking about your own climax, they will surely not return for more. Blaming your partner for taking longer to climb the stairs does not change the fact that she still wants to get to where you've only taken her part-way."

Bill O'Reilly swung his head around and scowled angrily at Pat Robertson while Dick Cheney pretended not to notice. In fact, he pretended not to know there was even a conversation going on at all.

"Where did you hear such nonsense? What would make you or anyone think a woman actually wants to do anything but please her man?"

"I heard it in one of those movies we watched when we first got here. I really didn't know what it meant and what fortune cookies had to do with it until Smokey explained it to me."

"Fortune cookies?"

Blade wasn't sure he was following, but needed to know as much as possible in case the old man's aphrodisiac was no longer available to him in the near future.

"Making sex is like a Chinese dinner: it ain't over 'til you both get your cookies."

Blade still wasn't sure he got the point until Pat Robertson clarified.

"Smokey says it's rude to have desert in front of someone else without making sure they get theirs too. We're supposed to share, not just take it all for ourselves."

Fung Wah interrupted by clearing his throat in yet another exaggerated theatrical production. The Three and Blade turned to see what the great wind was doing now.

"We have learned that our charge is in great danger. We must prepare to go up there tonight to bring the Wu to safety."

As he explained what Blade had told him about the plans Dr. Carlson had for Constance Void, Smokey wandered into the room wearing nothing but a towel around his waist. As much as Pat Robertson wanted to continue paying attention, it didn't take much temptation to shatter his willpower.

"Why wait until tonight?" Dick Cheney was all for charging in now and thinking about the consequences later. "If she is in danger, wouldn't it be best to get her out of there before any harm comes to her?"

The old man explained there would be fewer staff on duty at night, and going in under the cover of darkness would give them the advantage.

Blade had already decided to hack into the Pleasant Valley Sunday's internet connection and disrupt it, as well as any of the staff member's cell phones between the hours of midnight and eight AM. It would at least slow down anyone who might discover their patient's escape.

He could also reroute the center's phone lines so any staff that might try to call out will get an automated menu that plays perpetual elevator music and never connects them to a real person.

He was congratulating himself on all the things he'd learned since coming to America when Bill O'Reilly started blustering some nonsense about the minimum wage workers on duty at night in the clinic and how people like that don't deserve to call themselves Americans.

"Nephew, I think you've lost sight of who the real Bill O'Reilly is. Besides, we want those minimum wage workers to be doing a lax job so we can get the Wu out of there safely without being discovered. And let us not forget that our beloved Wu is an American. This country and its minimum wage workers did a good job of raising her and keeping her safe for us, including making sure she paid no attention to the nonsense spouted by the real Bill O'Reilly and Pat Robertson."

"What about Dick Cheney?"

Of course Bill O'Reilly was ever the watchful one on the lookout for the fault in another's argument. But it was only because he enjoyed exploiting them and claiming victory.

"Oh she paid very close attention to Dick Cheney, I promise you that. It was a necessary sacrifice, I assure you. Keeping an eye on any demon isn't for the faint of heart, and the Wu is anything but that."

"I have someone I can call who was made for this kind of thing," Smokey said.

The fact that anyone with such a perfectly hairless tattooed chest and impossibly tiny waist and hips could say anything to make himself even more irresistible seemed beyond the range of possibility to Pat Robertson. But when Smokey opened his mouth to finish the thought all he could think about was those lips pressed against the back of his neck.

"She's got a big truck and can get us out of there with this Wu of yours so your car isn't spotted by security cameras in the area."

Blade insisted Smokey use his encrypted phone, and told the others to stay off their own phones.

"From here on out, it's radio silence. Anything with a microphone has to go. No cell phones, no cordless phones, no Skype or computers with built-in microphones. All of them can make handy bugging devices for anyone with half my skills."

Bill O'Reilly and Dick Cheney nodded their understanding, but Pat Robertson only looked longingly in the direction of the other room, where Smokey had gone with Blade's phone.

By the time he returned the arrangements had been made. They would meet up at Point Mugu State Park near Malibu at one AM.

"She said she'll be coming back up from something she's got going in Venice, so this works for her. And she said she's got something she thinks will be of help, but she didn't say what it was."

It made Blade nervous. He was a man who didn't like surprises. But the rest of them were growing accustomed to celebrating the random, so looked forward to it.

CHAPTER SIXTEEN

"Call me Izmail."

The knife was dripping chocolate pudding all over her hair. But only because her hair had been shaved off and laid out neatly next to her bald head. Which was on the operating table she was strapped to.

Wait. That can't be right. Knives don't talk. And isn't the knife that's used in the Jewish circumcision ceremony called an Izmail?

It was then she realized the hand holding the knife could barely reach the table. The badly behaved Jewish midgets had found her. And they were about to circumcise her brain.

Constance Void turned to the man on the operating table to the right of hers. It was Haj. But it

was too late. The top of his skull was gone and a badly
behaved Jewish midget was pouring a bottle of pills
into his exposed brain.

"Jennn...air....eeeeeeeeekkk."

If that was how he thought a badly behaved
Jewish midget should pronounce the word *generic,*
someone needed to set him straight, because he
sounded like some kind of over-amped Frenchman on
meth. An over-amped badly behaved Jewish midget
Frenchman on meth. She wanted to tell him that,
wanted to spit the words into his face. But she couldn't.
He was a midget. He couldn't reach her face. Which
was why his little knife was doing all the talking.

*Isn't it just like a badly behaved Jewish midget to
let his knife do all the talking?*

She could hear muttering coming from her left,
but try as she might she couldn't take her eyes off Haj
and all those generic drugs being poured into his brain.
Until the sound of Jack Kerouac's voice finally broke
through clearly enough for her to realize he was on the
other operating table, the one to her left. He was
strapped down and his head had been shaved. A midget
riding on another midget's shoulders was sharpening
his knife and grinning while yet another midget ran
around the table singing a song from Fiddler on the
Roof.

*Or is it Yentl? Damn, maybe it's Jesus Christ
Superstar. And what was that in the little freak's*

hands?

He had an enormous plastic bottle with a label on it that said simply, *pills.*

As she struggled with the straps holding down her arms and legs, a sound began to drift through the window from outside. It was a curious buzzing which got louder and louder. It was filling the room and she finally realized it was the gardener with his leaf blower – and he was standing next to her.

"Quick. Hand me the pudding so I can load this thing."

As we often experience in dreams, the chocolate pudding simply appeared. But then again, isn't that always the way it is with chocolate pudding? The gardener dropped the cups of pudding down the chute of the leaf blower, and began firing it like some kind of missile launcher designed by a demented Betty Crocker. The midgets screamed and ran away in terror.

Who knew badly behaved Jewish midgets were afraid of chocolate pudding?

Constance Void opened her eyes. She lay there in the dim light that had only just begun drifting in from the reluctant dawn. Having the same dream three nights in a row was significant. Both nights she'd been at Pleasant Valley Sunday she'd dreamed it, and then there was the first time, the night before she went on the run from Chinese illegal organ traffickers.

The Void may not be a stickler for the rules, but

248

she always obeyed the rule of three. But it was only because it was one of the very few rules that actually made sense to her.

Deciding to ignore the clinic rule about no martial arts Constance slid into her red Chucks before padding down to the courtyard to do some T'ai Chi in the sunrise and get her head straight. Besides, it was Saturday morning. She doubted there would be any staff on duty that would really care if she performed a martial art in the courtyard or not. And surely she was the only patient who was up and around at Pleasant Valley Sunday this early in the morning. It was barely light.

Which was why it surprised her to see Haj, Jack Kerouac, Jerry Fletcher, Glenn Greenworld, and Carlos Castaneda sitting in the courtyard waiting for her as though she was late for a very important meeting.

Had she been the white rabbit, she would have looked at her oversized pocket watch and fretted about the time. But she wasn't the white rabbit, was she? One didn't need to go ask Alice who she was; it was perfectly clear she was Constance Void and she wasn't actually late. She was just the last patient to be driven out to the courtyard at dawn by a terrible dream involving midgets with sharp objects and chocolate pudding.

"At first I thought I was having the same old Moby Dick nightmare," Jack Kerouac said. "Until I realized there is never any pudding in that one. Nor are there gardeners with missile launching leaf blowers. Come to think of it, there are no midgets in that one either."

The group proceeded to share the details of the dream, comparing and contrasting those who saw themselves in the dream with the ones where they were merely a third person observer of it.

Constance had to admit, this group was not just more therapeutic, but far more productive than the one they had endured with old what's-her-name in the group therapy room yesterday.

She also had to admit it was pretty random only she, Jack Kerouac and Haj had dreamed they were actually in the dream as themselves. The others were merely third person observers, helpless to do anything but watch.

And while she ordinarily celebrated the random, Constance sensed this was one time when she needed to be more discerning and hold off putting on her party hat. When Haj spoke she knew she'd made the right decision.

"I do not know why the rest of you are all having this dream. I am the only one who has asked for the surgery. It makes no sense."

"Surgery?"

Carlos was recoiling at the word for reasons the others might never understand. They also might never understand why he was even in the courtyard with them, considering he was terrified of everyone there. But Constance Void understood perfectly well what he was doing there – and she was pleased. It was exactly where he needed to be. What's more, it was exactly where she needed him to be.

Haj explained the reason he had chosen the Pleasant Valley Sunday Rehabilitation and Psychiatric Treatment Center was due to the reputation Dr. Ben Carlson had for his groundbreaking psychosurgery.

"I worked so hard to achieve what I have. And none of it has been easy as a Muslim in America. Take my work teaching culinary arts at Ventura College, for instance. Do you have any idea what I had to go through just to keep my job after nine eleven?"

"Holy shit." Jerry abruptly cut Haj off. "I just did a search on Dr. Carlson and his psychosurgery and this is not good. Not good at all. Haj, tell me you didn't ask this guy to cut into your brain. Please."

But Haj couldn't tell him that because it would have been a lie. Not only had he asked Dr. Carlson for the surgery, but it was scheduled for Sunday morning.

"Tomorrow? But what about the things Morgan La Fay said here about magic curing madness when it's been caused by magic? Aren't you going to give her a chance to see if she can reverse the curse?"

Haj only hung his head and sat quietly. How could he make them understand he'd had enough and lost all hope? The surgery would silence the voices, and at this point that was all he cared about.

Constance understood, even if the others didn't. She knew what it meant to be at the end of one's rope and see the only option being the storm tossed rocks churning at the edge of that angry sea at the bottom of the cliff.

But she also knew what afflicted Haj was neither organic nor supernatural. It was man made. It was, in fact shenanigans; the worst kind of curse this world has ever known. She had spotted it the moment she first saw him and told herself she would do what was necessary to intervene.

"Wait. What time tomorrow?" She interrupted her own train of thought.

"What; the surgery?"

Constance nodded and he said it was at eight in the morning. The hair on her arms stood at attention as though a high ranking officer had just entered the barracks for a surprise inspection.

A staff member had cornered her after "dinner" the night before and told her the clinic needed some routine blood work on her for insurance purposes and she needed to fast after midnight. She had chuckled to herself about it because she'd pretty much been fasting since arriving. The "food" there gave her no other choice. The test was scheduled for eight in the morning on Sunday.

Jack Kerouac said the same staff member had told him the same thing. He was supposed to be at the clinic surgery at eight in the morning Sunday, which he thought odd at the time because they'd drawn his blood when he was admitted. He, Haj and Constance all looked at each other. How could a staff that wasn't even there attend to blood tests on two patients while a third one is having surgery? It made no sense.

"Unless all three of you have been scheduled for psychosurgery; which you have, if what I'm looking at on the clinic computer is correct."

He didn't like to brag, but his years of living online had taught Jerry how to get into most systems, and one of the things he'd been surprised to learn was just because a computer was turned off it didn't mean it couldn't be hacked. The CMOS battery gives a computer just enough power for any interested party to slide on in through that handy backdoor key, even when the computer is not turned on.

"Don't you see it, Haj?" Glenn pointed out the obvious as she crossed the courtyard and stood in front of him, pointing at Constance. "It's the magic she promised you. It's such a powerful magic that's been used against you it's taking the combined power of all of us to undo it. And that's why we've all had the dream. We need each other here. We need all our strengths, all our weaknesses; combined."

Carlos surprised everyone by contributing his

insights as an anthropologist, and it turned out to be the key they needed.

"I'll tell you what I know about midgets. They're the smallest of the men among us. And of course they're terrifying; that goes without saying. But if we set that aside for a moment and just look at what they symbolize in the dreams, because many cultures choose to consider the meaning of the symbols in their dreams rather than taking the dreams literally."

If only the religious fundamentalists would consider the same approach, we'd all be in for a lot less death, destruction, heartache and sexual victimization. Constance was once again letting her mind wander off topic.

"Midgets themselves are no more or less prone to corruption than anyone else; theoretically, of course. But when we think about what smallness symbolizes, what we mean when we say a man is *being small,* we invariably think of attributes like *corrupted, petty, greedy, narcissistic, selfish, heartless* and even *psychopathic.*"

Not only had Constance Void known Carlos Castaneda was exactly where he needed to be, she was confident in his input as an anthropologist. She'd been entertaining the thought that perhaps the pantheist would completely overcome his xenophobia and return to a productive life if she got him away from the television, and in particular, from Flocks News. And it appeared she had been right.

It seemed the vitriolic talking heads at that intellect crushing television network had succeeded in blocking his valuable input with the fear they'd induced. Constance knew better than anyone how much they all needed that input. It was helping them to focus on the fact that a small man corrupted by an addiction to sweet rewards was planning to circumcise not just her brain, but that of Haj and Jack Kerouac as well on Sunday morning. Tomorrow was Sunday.

Constance Void had no way of knowing Dr. Carlson was selecting patients for psychosurgery based on emojis he was collecting. She had never engaged in any kind of online social networking and therefore had no idea what an emoji was. So she had no reason to know research by neuroscientists had shown emojis trigger the same pleasure center in the brain as sweets. Sweets like chocolate pudding. But then again, with her wireless connection and apparent Faraday Bubble, it's entirely possible Constance Void was as adept at navigating the electronic superhighway as Jerry Fletcher, only she did it invisibly. Without the bow tie. Or maybe with one. If it was invisible, how would anybody know?

With all deference to Carlos Castaneda's fear of martial arts, she led the group in a session of T'ai Chi to help them all feel centered, and although Carlos did not participate, he didn't run away either.

Providing some valuable input in the discussion about midgets and symbolism in dreams had returned a feeling to the anthropologist he hadn't known for a long time. If there was even the slightest chance the group might need some more of that valuable input, he wasn't going to miss the opportunity.

Constance was lost in that place of non-thought one often finds oneself in at sunrise when engaging in a contemplative exercise like T'ai Chi when she spotted Suzanne standing at the edge of the courtyard. Even the shadows cast by the overhang above her couldn't hide the fact she had been crying.

Not only were her eyes swollen, but her ordinarily pale complexion had turned an ashen gray which only seemed to accentuate the redness around them.

First Constance, and then the rest of the group stopped and turned to watch as Carlos stood from the planter where he sat and walked over to the woman.

"So which were you; observer, or midget?" He took her hand and guided her gently to a wrought iron chair.

"Neither. I was Izmail."

Suzanne described the exact same scene in the operating room, complete with the midget running around singing a song from Yentl. At which point an argument erupted between the others about which song was in their dream and which musical it was from.

It would have continued to go on too, if Suzanne hadn't startled them all by putting two fingers to her lips and blowing an ear piercing whistle to get their attention. When she saw their surprise, she shrugged. It was just one of those things she knew how to do before she was reborn in Christ and submitted to His Divine Plan of headship. At which time the men stopped letting her do things; although she couldn't quite remember why they made her stop whistling.

"Why was I the knife?"

"Because you're a tool."

Suzanne barely heard Glenn's reply. She couldn't take her eyes off the superhero's armpits. If Constance Void hadn't told her about the origin of the unusual crow's nest tattoos, she wouldn't be able to make any sense whatsoever of what the superhero who points had under her arms.

"I'm a tool. I don't even know what that means."

"It means you probably take a lot of Ambien to go with that expensive ring you've got on your finger. Do you even know why they call them blood diamonds? I bet you've got a Bible in the pocket of your lab coat, haven't you?"

"I'm not getting your point."

Glenn wasn't sure if the licensed marriage and family therapist was being deliberately obtuse or not.

"Didn't Dr. Carlson tell you the only way to

help your client here is to perform a radical psychosurgery on her?"

Suzanne nodded and Glenn crossed the courtyard, sat on the ground in front of her and crossed her legs. To the others she looked more like the yogi who points than the superhero who points. But she explained things like a boss.

"Is that what you truly, genuinely, in the very bottom of your professionally trained heart think she needs? I mean, from what I understand about the procedure, it sounds like an extreme form of lobotomy. There's no going back from there. Your client won't get a do-over. What exactly is she doing that makes you think that's what she needs?"

"So you're saying I'm a tool because I'm letting the doctor use me for some agenda of his own."

Glenn nodded and Suzanne saw all the others nod in agreement with her.

"But what about demonic possession; how do you expect him to use the standard model of psychotherapy and psychotropic drugs on something like that?"

The pitch of her voice was climbing higher. Rather than match that pitch, Carlos spoke in a steady, soothing voice as he explained.

"We expect him to behave like a man of science. And as a man of science myself, I think it's only appropriate to questions his methods. For one thing, did you ask yourself why he scheduled these procedures on a Sunday, when the clinic is empty of any professional staff who might observe him and have questions?"

Suzanne's eyes widened and what little color had returned to her face drained out again.

"Wait. Who is he performing surgery on this Sunday?" She sounded clearly alarmed. "I thought you were talking about the conversation I had with him about Constance yesterday. He told me it might be an option for her, but we haven't spoken since."

"Who is Constance?"

Jack Kerouac wished he'd brought paper and a pen with him to take notes. Suzanne shot a helpless look at the Void, who shrugged her shoulders and nodded her head.

"If you haven't figured it out by now, her name isn't Zann Killjoy and I'm not Morgan La Fay. We got into a spot of trouble up in the 'Nard and found ourselves on the run from Chinese illegal organ traffickers. Suzanne Shill here, who really is a licensed marriage and family therapist, did some quick thinking and checked me in to Pleasant Valley Sunday under an assumed name."

"The 'Nard?"

Jack Kerouac was determined to remember the dialogue until he got back to the typewriter in his room.

"Oxnard."

Glenn, Jerry and Suzanne all said it in a perfect chorus. A ripple of infectious giggling broke out and it seemed none of them had been vaccinated against it.

Like any ripple, it grew exponentially, elevating a mood that could easily be weighed down otherwise. News that the one person a group of people trusts implicitly has been lying to them about something as fundamental as their name can do that.

"Okay people, no fair confusing the Muslim foreigner." Even Haj was giggling. "We need to start calling people and places by their rightful names."

The Void bowed ceremoniously.

"Constance Void; at your service. And everything else I've told you is true. I really am an Absurdist Voodoo Priestess and I really did call forth Edward Snowden's selfless act of courage with chocolate pudding and a leaf blower."

"You did what?" Suzanne shrieked. "When did this happen? No wonder Dr. Carlson wants to dissect your brain!"

"I think the more important question is why anyone would name a city after a large farm animal with a bad cold," Jerry said. Constance pointed out that the founders of the City of Oxnard weren't the only ones confused about large farm animals.

"Large farm animals are called beasts of burden because of the heavy work they do, like pulling the farmer's plow, right? So have you ever listened to that Rolling Stones song where he sings *I'll Never Be Your Beast of Burden* and asked yourself why he's promising someone he won't be their large farm animal?

I mean, come on. He keeps talking about wanting to make love in the same song where he talks about large farm animals. Am I the only one who finds this disturbing?"

She was looking around the courtyard at the men, mostly – and each of them was squirming. Except Haj, who just didn't get it.

Jack Kerouac was fairly certain he was never going to get over having not brought anything to write with, and promised himself he would never make that mistake again.

But leave it to the xenophobic pantheist to be the voice of reason in the group. Carlos patiently pointed out the only truly pertinent question any of them should be asking was what they were going to do about the doctor's plans to perform his brain circumcision on three patients back-to-back the very next day.

"That's just your opinion," Jerry snapped, which was uncharacteristic of him, but his blood sugar was getting low. A diet of nothing but a sugary nutritional supplement will do that.

Carlos had often wondered why people would say *that's just your opinion* when someone stated the obvious. They were especially inclined to say it if they disagreed with the obvious, even when the obvious was factual.

He couldn't count the number of times he'd said something patently obvious to a person like, "If you're not careful you might fall in that hole we just dug," only to be told that was just his opinion. Of course, it always amused him when that person then fell in the hole. When they complained about getting hurt he would then tell them it was just their opinion.

But Glenn offered another perspective when she pointed out it couldn't hurt to also ask themselves why Dr. Carlson was targeting a writer, an Absurdist Voodoo Priestess and a community college teacher of culinary arts who happened to be a Muslim.

"I mean, think about it. Of the three of them, only Haj is hearing voices. Jack isn't even here as a mental patient, for crying out loud. And Morg...Const....whatever your name is, is perfectly lucid. So why them?"

Suzanne thought she may have an idea why her client was chosen. "Constance, did you meet with Dr. Carlson yesterday?" The Void nodded and gave her a thumbnail sketch of how the meeting went.

"Did you say anything about your incantation with the pudding in that meeting?"

"No, but I talked about it in group therapy yesterday, why?"

"He was already inclined to think you were possessed by Satan, just from the conversation we had. If he heard you were practicing any kind of magic or sorcery, it would be enough to convince him to take extreme measures. But he said nothing to me about it at all. And he certainly didn't tell me he'd scheduled three surgeries at once, with no staff in attendance."

Jerry wasn't sure if maybe it was just his blood sugar dipping too low, but he was confused. He had that discomforting feeling he was the only one there who didn't understand what was going on.

"I don't get it. What's demonic about magic?"

Constance Void smiled reassuringly and shook her head.

"Nothing. The reason all forms of "magic" are branded "of the devil" by religious leaders is to keep people focused on a narrow religious perspective, made narrow deliberately so you don't expand your mind enough to think your way out of that narrow channel, which is really nothing more than a mental trap.

Religious leaders are no different than the average televangelist: they need to keep you tuned in to their program to milk you for as much as they can. The truth is, magic is magic, neither good nor bad. Just like pudding, it all depends on how you use it. You can put the pudding on your thighs, or you can put it on their shiny things. It's all up to you. Free will – ain't it a bitch?"

Haj seemed to have been animated by what the Void was saying and scowled. "But even the Quran states that magic is an act of blasphemy!"

"If that were true, Haj, then cursing someone for being homosexual would be blasphemy. Religious leaders, politicians, even the good Doctor Carlson here openly curse gays every day of the week, insisting they are damned for eternity. Then they go a step further and curse the entire human community for daring to allow gays to live among them as equals.

Where I come from that's a curse; the very worst kind of magic. And they justify practicing that kind of magic by favoring one Biblical edict over another. Cherry picking like that is not only intellectually sloppy, it's suspect."

"How do you know Dr. Carlson is opposed to homosexuality?"

Suzanne seemed almost as confused as Jerry, whose face had gone pale and hands had begun to shake. Constance knew they had to wrap things up and get him to the cafeteria before his blood sugar dipped any lower.

"You're not the only one who's read the man's published works. I take it you missed the one about using his psychosurgery to "cure" homosexuality. Now let's go eat. We can continue this over breakfast. There's food-like substances to be eaten, and plans to be made."

Jack Kerouac was relieved. It would give him a chance to stop by his room and grab a pen and notepad. After the conversation he'd had the night before with Constance Void, and now with the others, he was feeling the story coming on. The one that would be fact stranger than fiction, written as fiction.

And there would be midgets. And pudding, damnit. Chocolate pudding.

But Suzanne was still puzzling over the doctor's decision to circumcise her client's brain. What possible threat could Constance Void be to a man as powerful and successful as Dr. Carlson?

After all, her name isn't Cassandra; it's Constance. She isn't some freaking oracle from Delphi. Are fundamentalists really that threatened by the thought of a woman having the gift of prophecy?

CHAPTER SEVENTEEN

The thing that puzzled Toole most was the Chinese and Mossad seemed to be at odds with each other's agenda. And try as he might, he couldn't wrap his head around the conflict, considering the Chinese are Israel's largest trading partner in Asia.

If it wasn't for the enterprising Israelis, the kosher food industry in China would collapse, considering how many Israeli firms have set up shop there. Perhaps the data in Constance Void's brain contained some recipe an algorithm has predicted will be invented for the perfect gluten free matzo balls.

Undoubtedly the Chinese wanted the data stored in Constance Void's brain, whatever it was. Was it possible Mossad was manipulating Dr. Ben Carlson to cut that data out of her brain? If so, could it mean the Void had data that threatened the Israelis? Did it have anything to do with the gluten free kosher food industry?

Thinking about matzo balls made Toole think about matzo ball soup, which naturally led to thinking about egg flower soup. That of course made him realize he was hungry again.

Judging from the seismic magnitude of his hunger pangs, Toole decided he needed something substantial. And he knew exactly what that something would be.

Leaving his cubicle, he headed north toward Lankershim Boulevard with only minutes to spare before the only place on Earth for a decent burger would be closing at half past one.

He was the last customer of the night, and yet the smiling face at the drive-up window was as fresh and delightful as their food. Times like these all Toole could think was *God bless America.*

Pulling out of the In N Out drive-up with a Double-Double and fries, plus one of their incomparable chocolate shakes, Toole decided to head home and eat on his balcony in NoHo. His hipster neighbors were bound to be sleeping by then, so there was little risk of being subjected to their Arcade Fires, Strokes or Vampire Weekends.

Why anyone would want to spend a weekend

among vampires was beyond Toole. And the only person he'd ever known to have a stroke never recovered the ability to speak, so he really couldn't see what the fascination was with them, either.

As for the arcade fires, Toole made a point of listening to the police band frequently for any calls involving arson at video arcades. While he hadn't heard anything yet, he was confident when it happened the culprits would be living right next door.

It had been too long since he'd been home. Some food and a shower was all it took to convince him it had also been too long since he'd slept, and a little shut eye would probably be just what he needed to put the whole thing together. Somewhere in all the puzzle pieces he'd collected since sitting there in that courtroom in Ventura, there was a crystal clear big picture staring down at him as he stretched out on his bed and shut his eyes. And he was certain that big picture would illustrate an unholy alliance the likes of which the U.S. had never seen.

At first he thought he was with his mother watching King of Hearts. Every year on Christmas Eve they would sit together and enjoy their favorite film while eating pretzels and string cheese. The story of the little French town in World War One seemed to resonate with both of them for some reason. Abandoned by everyone except the residents of the insane asylum when the German army sets a bomb to blow it up, a Scottish soldier is sent into the little town to diffuse the explosive. Only he doesn't know the people he encounters are from the asylum.

And neither did Toole when he encountered those same characters in the dream he was having. The Chinese were on one side of the street and Mossad was on the other, leaving Toole and the mental patients in the middle of the street, surrounded. The situation seemed hopeless, and nothing the mental patients did to defend themselves made any sense.

One woman just stood there pointing. Another kept shouting trivial facts in 140 characters or less while another just stood there taking notes about what a great story this was going to make. Just when Toole thought it was hopeless, Roz and a Rastafarian showed up with leaf blowers and chocolate pudding saying, *who has the duct tape, we have to hurry because the midgets are coming.*

Death Cab for Cutie was singing "I'll Follow You Into the Dark," and all Toole could think was how much he hated emo when he realized it was coming through the wall. It was dawn and as he lay in the thin morning light he realized he hadn't been able to avoid the hipsters after all.

He needed coffee and possibly another shower, but more than anything he needed to get out of his apartment before his neighbors began playing Airborne

Toxic Event. Toole was understandably terrified of breathing in any of that.

He toyed with the idea of going next door and promising to bring them the perfect recipe for gluten free matzo balls if they would stop playing their hipster music until he left for work. Maybe it might buy him some time to make a nice pot of Kona roast and put some thought into that dream he'd just had.

But after several minutes of taking only shallow breaths he opted for Peet's Coffee. They were on Westwood and he'd pass right by there on his way back to the office.

All the way there he puzzled over the dream, which was more vivid than most of his dreams. But by the time he got back to his cubicle his attention quickly turned to something he hadn't noticed the night before. Dr. Carlson wasn't just performing psychosurgery on Constance Void the following day, he was performing it on two other patients as well.

Not only that, but one of the patients wasn't even there for psychiatric treatment. He was a garden variety alcoholic, there for rehab. It made no sense. Since when was rearranging the brain with a scalpel considered an accepted treatment for alcoholism? Wouldn't it leave the patient almost as dysfunctional as he was when he was drunk all the time? And then there was the third patient. He was a harmless culinary arts instructor at the college. With no family history of mental illness and no history of drugs or alcohol, the devout forty year old Muslim had abruptly started hearing voices telling him horrible things.

About himself.

Toole wondered if the man also had some data stored in his brain that somebody wanted, somebody who knew the only way to retrieve it was to cut it out. Was that what the mysterious emojis on Dr. Carlson's computer were all about?

Because he'd spent so much time away from the office he had a lot of data to review and catch up on, and it took most of the day. He'd already listened to the meetings Dr. Carlson had with both Suzanne Shill and then with Constance Void.

Toole could clearly see where the doctor felt threatened by the Void's confidence. Men of his religious persuasion usually do feel threatened by confident women, and tend to deal with that threat the only way they know how: through domination. He couldn't think of a better way to dominate a woman than to neuter her brain surgically; especially a woman like Constance Void.

He'd also already reviewed the group therapy meeting, where he'd gotten that important puzzle piece involving Constance Void's connection to GWEN towers decorated in chocolate pudding. But he could have paid a little more attention to the part where she described the equipment she used for it. It might have cleared up some confusion for him later that night.

Of course, Toole was most intrigued by the Void's late night visit to the day room. He was especially glad Jack Kerouac had smuggled his own cell phone in with him when he was admitted. It made listening to conversations in both the day room and out in the courtyard almost too easy.

He found the conversation with the alcoholic writer out in the courtyard especially interesting and made a note to look up any data he could find on the friend he claimed had been working as a data technician and archivist. Perhaps Toole might be able to make an educated guess about which private security firm he'd been working for and who might have been involved in his murder.

One of the things that made his work so time-consuming was the fact he couldn't just follow Constance Void's own cell phone data stream since there was none.

He had to review the feed for each cell phone and laptop of those around her and hope it had an encounter with the Void in its data.

Because he couldn't physically be at his desk for cast-iron coverage of each cell phone, he had to resort to reviewing their feed after the fact. Without question, it was a long, slow, laborious process.

The life of a data analyst is not one that would ever make it onto the silver screen, largely because they spend most of their time in front of the small one peering at entirely uninteresting bits of data.

By the time he was finished reviewing all the pertinent data from the clinic starting with the moment the two women arrived Thursday night, and leading up to that morning, the daylight was beginning to fade and Toole was just getting caught up.

He'd been browsing through the doctor's notes a little more and looking at the schedule when it occurred to him there wouldn't be any staff on duty except for a skeleton crew all weekend. The doctor wanted to be alone in that surgery with those three patients. It made the hair on the back of his neck stand up. He was curious to know if all three patients even knew the surgery was planned for them.

Leaving the familiarity of the clinic computer system he accessed that morning's data stream on all available cell phones. He was surprised to discover when he listened to Jack Kerouac's that Suzanne Shill and Constance Void had come clean with the patients about their real reasons for being at Pleasant Valley Sunday. And it all came out as they were discussing a dream they had all shared the night before. It wasn't exactly the same dream Toole had, but the similarities, including the pudding and leaf blowers and midgets made him nervously tap his toe beneath his desk.

He'd been assured that by signing a non-disclosure agreement about certain trade secrets developed by the

Defense Department Toole would be spared ever being subjected to having the technology used on him. Yet something was making him feel paranoid about having the same dreams a bunch of crazy people in a mental hospital were having.

Wishing he'd picked up something to eat when he was getting that coffee, Toole considered briefly driving back over to the In N Out for another Double-Double, but told himself his work came first.

So he wandered into the break room for the last cup of pudding he'd left in the fridge and smiled at a passing thought of Roz as he pulled off the foil top and returned to his desk. He was licking the first bite off the plastic spoon while watching the group of patients in the cafeteria on the surveillance camera feed from that morning while simultaneously listening in on their conversation through the cell phone feed.

They were discussing their plans, since they knew three of them were in mortal danger of having their brains circumcised. Chuckling to himself that Constance Void would call the surgery a circumcision, he had just put his feet up on his desk and settled in for the duration of their conversation when the feed from the camera went dead. Moments later the cell phone feed was dead, too.

Dead. As in no longer streaming. But not just no longer streaming; no longer in the database.

No matter how hard he tried, nothing Toole did

enabled him to access the data feed again. It was blocked, and whoever had done it was far more sophisticated than he was in managing code, because he could find no way around the wall that had just gone up. It wasn't just a firewall, it was an impenetrable wall that stretched farther than he'd ever seen. It blocked his access at every turn.

He sat there thinking about walls and what he knew about them when he was abruptly reminded of one wall in particular – The Great Firewall of China.

The Chinese had blocked his access to the data feed streaming from Pleasant Valley Sunday. There was absolutely no doubt in his mind about it. Only the Chinese would have such advanced computer skills.

Every fiber of his being told Toole it meant they were planning on making their move well in advance of both the surgery and whatever it was Mossad had up its sleeve.

He had no choice but to head up to Ventura County and hope none of the interested parties knew he was involved, since he fully planned to stake out the clinic in Camarillo.

And maybe drive by the apartment of a certain pretty bailiff in Ventura while he was up there. Come to think of it, he remembered seeing an In N Out just off the 101 between Camarillo and Ventura.

Just to be on the safe side, Toole decided it might be best to take one of the fleet cars. A nondescript gray Sebring with government plates would be less likely to draw attention from anyone who might question him sitting outside the treatment center in Camarillo. Or outside an apartment complex in Ventura.

Deciding finally to simply head north long before the Dodger game got out and brought the freeway to a standstill, Toole found himself pulling out of the Oxnard In N Out less than ninety minutes after leaving the NSA fleet parking lot. Glancing at his Double-Double, fries and chocolate shake, he only wished they served chocolate pudding.

Chocolate pudding and Roz had been all that seemed to be on his mind the entire drive up the 101. Considering it was still way too early to stake out the clinic in Camarillo, Toole decided he had no reason not to head into Ventura and eat his In N Out sitting outside Roz Ferriday's apartment.

But he'd barely finished chewing his first bite of burger when he saw her come out of her apartment building. She was carrying what looked like a case of chocolate pudding in a cup and got into a taco truck parked on a side street after putting them in the back.

Did Roz have a side job Toole knew nothing about? One that involved selling Mexican food at night? Is there a big demand for chocolate pudding with tacos? If so, why had she been throwing them away in her courtroom?

Toole had too many questions. He had no choice but to follow her. She was, after all, Roz of the halo eyes and trash can full of uneaten pudding, and most recently of the taco truck. The woman who'd stolen his heart.

Luckily, Toole was quite accomplished at eating In N Out while driving, as are most self-respecting natives of Southern California. But following the taco truck was making him wish he'd gotten Mexican food instead.

And chocolate pudding.

What Toole didn't know was there are perks that tend to come with Roz's job. The owner of the taco truck had been ticketed for having no auto insurance so many times his food truck was impounded. But how is anyone supposed to get auto insurance without an American driver's license?

It was an argument he made successfully to Roz in the parking lot of the courthouse and she agreed to help him out by pushing his paperwork through showing him as the owner of the taco truck but someone else entirely as the only authorized driver.

Of course, that authorized driver was Roz, who had no trouble getting insurance on the taco truck. So she kept the taco truck in her neighborhood and drove it to the corner of Ventura Avenue and Fifth Street every weekday morning, where the grateful father of four had his oldest son drive her to work and bring her back at the end of the day. And each morning as his son drove Roz to work she ate the breakfast he brought for her – his mother's legendary tamales dulces.

Toole tried not to follow too closely, and at first it appeared Roz was headed for Oxnard when she drove down Victoria Avenue and turned onto Channel Islands Boulevard. It made perfect sense to Toole that she would be taking a taco truck to Oxnard. Any time of night.

But curiously, it turned out she was headed for Pacific Coast Highway. For the first time, it occurred to the NSA analyst that he should have put the pretty bailiff under electronic surveillance. But Toole had considered himself above stooping to what so many others in the intelligence industry did in their spare time. He wanted to manage this courtship the old fashioned way. Hence sitting outside her apartment and tailing her down PCH.

CHAPTER EIGHTEEN

Blade had no doubt it was his employers who had cut the data feed from the Pleasant Valley Sunday Rehabilitation and Psychiatric Treatment Center. He also had no doubt they'd discovered the same thing he had about the true identity of the woman Fung Wah had asked him to keep an eye on.

What he didn't know was why they had been looking into it at all. Had they been monitoring him all along? Watching over his shoulder as he went about the business of hacking into things they themselves were paying him to hack into?

If so, it meant they had been aware of every single side job he'd taken over the years he'd been working for the Party. Including the ones for which he was paid in aphrodisiac. As a lightning bolt of fear surged through him, it lodged in his left kidney and he flinched. Not because it hurt, but because the thought of losing it did.

He backtracked through the steps he'd taken just before the feed was cut to see if he could spot any evidence they were there. First he had hacked into the server and routed all the incoming and outgoing data through a proxy server he had access to. He sent a code to the server to gradually slow the feed to a crawl and finally just stop. Then he programmed the outgoing phone lines so anyone trying to call out would reach a recording that was nothing but an infinite loop of caller options.

Basically, he just duplicated what Comcast's customers get when they call for help with their predictably unreliable service. After that, he settled in to watch the data feed get gradually lighter and lighter.

At least, that was what he expected to see, not an abrupt end to the data stream altogether. And he certainly didn't expect the firewall that suddenly appeared out of nowhere. It was blocking his access to any of the usual routes he took when he occasionally came up against resistance to his intrusions.

Blade knew of very few hackers with the skills to carry off that swift and impenetrable an intercept, and had an idea where he might be able to verify just who it was.

On a back channel in the *deep web* sits an innocuous chatroom where members discuss chess and other games of skill and strategy. If it was the one person Blade suspected might be involved, he wouldn't be able to resist bragging about it. It was his greatest weakness. And it was the reason Blade never missed the opportunity to play Texas Hold'em with him. It wasn't so much the guy had tells, it was his overinflated ego. It made him one giant walking tell.

It didn't take long in the chatroom to confirm his suspicions, and to learn that it was indeed his own government who had placed the order to cut the data stream of some mental health facility in Camarillo none of them had ever heard of except Blade.

When he saw the words "dissident" and "enemy of the state" were being used to justify the black-op scheduled to go down before dawn involving one of the patients at that facility, he knew the Wu had been targeted for elimination. But oddly, he also noticed something else that he didn't quite know what to make of.

There was a general warning being passed around among all the Chinese hackers in the chatroom and word had it that it came directly from their government: they were all to be on the lookout for Mossad and their friends. *Their friends?* Everybody knows Israel doesn't have any friends. They have allies and business partners. But friends? That word alone could result in losing hours to a discussion in the chatroom on the meaning of the word friendship. Something was going down, and though nobody knew what it was, they knew it was big.

When Blade called the herb shop, Fung Wah picked up before it got through the first ring. His voice was crisp and unnatural.

"Fung Wah's herb shop."

"Good evening, Master Herbalist. Traffic is thick tonight because of the big game. We should leave earlier than we had planned for the Mahjong tournament so we don't miss out on drawing our tiles."

"Our friend who likes sickly farm animals has a friend we're meeting up with, I will see if he can arrange for us to meet them earlier."

"Why don't you wait until I pick you up to do that?" Blade didn't want Smokey to risk using the shop phone to call his contact in Ventura County, and hoped he'd wait until he could use Blade's encrypted phone.

"We'll have a better idea of when we'll be arriving once we get past the 405 and traffic thins out. I will see you some time before ten."

Of course he knew they would be driving up Pacific Coast Highway, and wouldn't be anywhere near the 405. And he knew Fung Wah knew it too. But he hoped whoever was listening in on their conversation didn't, and that was what really mattered.

Blade arrived at the herb shop a little before ten, hoping it would give Smokey plenty of time to call his contact and bump up their meeting to midnight. By the time his friend got them from Malibu to Camarillo it would be close to one AM, maybe even later depending on traffic. More than anything, he wanted to get to the Wu before the Chinese operatives arrived. Blade wasn't eager to run up against those operatives. The Chinese government was known to use a variety of assassins, and all of them terrified Blade. Especially the ones with sharp utensils.

Knives and swords were the hacker's greatest fear, which would make his choice in names seem odd, unless you take into consideration his reasoning. When the Chinese government stationed the hacker in America he decided on the name as a sort of self-styled immersion therapy. Unfortunately, it hadn't worked. He was as terrified of blades as ever. Sometimes phobias are best left in the hands of professionals. Of course, Constance Void would tell him to be very careful around any professionals who utilize Neuro Linguistic Programming for phobias. Not all of them are working to eliminate them.

Fung Wah was deep in meditation when he arrived. Blade wondered how the old man could be so calm in the face of the danger they were about to confront. But perhaps the aging herbalist found some kind of solace in his incense and smoldering smudge sticks. At least the three nephews and the one with smoke colored eyes seemed to be in touch with reality. They explained there was too much of a risk their uncle's car had been identified in the Krispy Kreme parking lot, so preferred to take Blade's car.

It was the difference between there being plenty of room for everyone in Fung Wah's enormous Lincoln and squeezing all of them into a little Scion that only seated four passengers.

But Pat Robertson was more than happy to have Smokey sit on his lap, so it was settled. At shortly before half past ten Fung Wah slid into the front passenger seat as his nephews and Pat Robertson's dance partner made themselves comfortable in the back seat. The uncle couldn't help but notice Pat Robertson seemed to be almost too comfortable.

If it had been up to Dick Cheney, who even later insisted it was the right thing to do, they would have gotten on the 710 to Long Beach and then found themselves intractably stuck in post-Dodger game traffic trying to get to Pacific Coast Highway.

Bill O'Reilly took Dick Cheney's side and angrily insisted theirs actually made it a majority vote because Smokey and Blade's votes didn't count. Also, he claimed his blustering doubled the value of their votes against Fung Wah and Pat Robertson.

"And just why don't Smokey and Blade's votes

count?" Fung Wah very much regretted asking within minutes but by then it was too late.

"Because they're outsiders," Bill O'Reilly shouted, which in a car that small made everyone's ears ring. But Bill O'Reilly had long ago stopped caring how his shouting affected others, or even whether he made any sense.

It was perfectly self-evident that any opinion Bill O'Reilly had was absolutely reasonable even if it wasn't logical and therefore not just the only opinion that mattered, but the only one that was right and so he was justified in shouting it.

While ordinarily Pat Robertson would go along with anything Bill O'Reilly had to say, he was far too lost in Smokey's eyes to even care. Some things are just more important than Bill O'Reilly's twisted attempts to subvert the democratic process. Or Dick Cheney's. Bill O'Reilly remained certain for the rest of the night that when this whole thing was over, exit polls would show they were right all along.

It was Blade who won out when he simply stayed on surface streets and took Westwood all the way to Santa Monica, thus connecting to PCH effortlessly. Dick Cheney and Bill O'Reilly sulked angrily the entire way, which surprised no one.

They were still sulking when they arrived at Point Mugu State Park, and exited the cramped little car noisily, making sure everyone knew they hadn't let go of the argument. Except for Pat Robertson and Smokey, all were happy to be stretching their legs. The two young lovers seemed perfectly content to stay in the car. As is the case with most young lovers, cramped places do have their appeal.

The full moon had risen during their drive and hung just over the Pacific, a movie set floodlight reflecting in the water gently lapping the shore. Somewhere out in the spring calm surf a cadre of set lighting technicians were stationed on surfboards balancing a giant polished mirror between them, hoping they'd be earning overtime pay.

It was the kind of night where one would expect to find a carload of middle aged stoners parked facing the beach as they listen to Jack Johnson while smoking TrainWreck and discussing full moons and infinity and Bill Nye's denial of the universe's omniscience.

Only Blade kept an eye out for their connection, having long since grown accustomed to the moon upstaging all the players in Southern California.

Growing nervous when his friend hadn't arrived by one AM, he was about to resort to using his cell phone to call when he spotted a taco truck approach from the south. As Roz turned into the parking lot and pulled up next to his car, he noticed another vehicle approach from the south and pull over to the shoulder where it sat idling.

"Get in. I think we've picked up a tail." She had. Of that Blade was certain.

"It's a Sebring; with government plates."

"Which one?" Fung Wah said as he pulled Smokey Methson and Pat Robertson apart and shoved them into the back of the taco truck.

"Which what?"

There were times it seemed to Blade the imminently wise master herbalist had to be just playing dumb.

"Which government?"

Blade had to explain only members of the U.S. government drove the gray nondescript Sebring sedan, due to some curious contract with the manufacturer nobody could ever really figure out. Not even the American government. Nor did they know how to get out of the contract, especially since Chrysler had discontinued the model years earlier.

Assuming the CIA was on to them, he told Roz to keep an eye out for Mossad, who would undoubtedly be close behind. Largely because wherever the CIA went, Mossad was invariably close behind.

"But they won't be driving a Sebring."

"What about the MSS?" Fung Wah still seemed to be asking pointless questions as Roz expertly pulled the taco truck out onto PCH and checked her rear view mirror.

"We won't see The Chinese government's operatives coming until they're on top of us."

Blade was trying to assure him, but it really was no assurance at all. He considered explaining that no self-respecting member of Chinese intelligence would drive a Chrysler, nor would Israeli intelligence for that matter.

But he didn't think it would do anything to relieve the tension to explain the various intelligence agencies' preferences for automobiles. Besides, he was more curious to know who the black man with the dreadlocks sitting in the front passenger seat was.

"Something told me we'd be needing the Rastafarians." Roz nodded toward the space right behind the passenger seat and said one of the duffel bags had his kettle drum. "It's why I was so slow getting here. Had to drive down to Venice Beach to pick him up."

She didn't seem in any hurry to tell them his name, which was fine with Blade because he was more curious to know what was in the other canvas bag.

"That's the surprise I told you about. I've been knitting these caps in my spare time for a while now. And to really make them pop, I weave in this gorgeous fine copper thread. The Rastafarians sell them for me in Venice. In fact, they're all wearing them now. I call them Ferriday Caps. Go ahead, try them on; all of you. I insist."

Smokey eagerly pulled open the canvas bag and poured the contents out on the floor of the taco truck. The brightly colored caps tumbled out and the copper thread reflected the light of oncoming cars.

He watched as Bill O'Reilly and Dick Cheney each slipped one on and then he and Pat Robertson gently caressed each other's cheek putting them on each other. Fung Wah handed one to Blade, but did not put one on himself.

"What? You want me to put this on you? Because dude, I don't have those kind of feelings for you. No offense."

Fung Wah only shook his head and explained to Blade that neither he nor Constance Void would be needing any help bringing the Wu that night. Blade completely understood, but had no idea what had compelled Roz to make the caps and bring them with her. What exactly was Smokey's connection to her?

For the first time Smokey explained what he was doing in the Oxnard jail the night he met Pat Robertson, and how his long and winding road had led to his friendship with the officer of the court.

Port Hueneme, like most cities and towns across America, had been saturated with methamphetamines as a result of law enforcement's war on marijuana. Which of course was due to the private prison industry's need for bodies to fill their beds.

It made no sense to any of them until he explained further. Because there were far more marijuana users than meth users, when law enforcement would apprehend someone in possession of meth, they would make a bargain with him: give them the names of three marijuana users and they could go free.

The game of *Give Three Go Free* had proven to be remarkably profitable for law enforcement, whose funding depended on showing a robust drug arrest record. Three arrests for pot got them far more funding than one arrest for meth.

As well, prosecutors earned the attention they needed to bolster their political careers with so many convictions for pot. And of course the private prisons-for-profit made a fortune on the harmless pot smokers, who tended to be more peaceful than other felons.

Meanwhile, the meth users, who for the most part were also meth dealers, were being let back out into the community. Where they happily went about the business of saturating cities and towns across America with a drug that not only destroys some pretty important parts of the brain, like the amygdla, but leaves users unsuitable for anything but invariable prison sentences themselves. As violent offenders. That and a lifelong prescription of various generic drugs to counter the permanent effects of the meth, of course.

All at the American taxpayer expense, who doesn't benefit from any of it at all. Ever.

"I'm not seeing how that connects you to Roz."

Bill O'Reilly was speaking a little too loudly again and was beginning to get his angry voice back. At any moment he could launch into a tirade about drug use and how anyone who uses any drug at all belonged in prison and should permanently lose the right to vote.

Blade would then most likely consider asking him if he ever used alcohol, and then pointlessly ignite Bill O'Reilly's anger by reminding him that alcohol is a drug that can be just as dangerous as meth and cause devastation to the brain as well.

"By the time I was born Port Hueneme was saturated with meth. And just like so many of my friends and classmates, I was dealing it by the time I was in middle school. I made it to my eighteenth birthday before I was arrested for it, which surprised me and everyone else. And when I got the notice to appear in court, the wrong courtroom had been printed on the notice.

That's when I first met Roz; sitting in the wrong courtroom all day. She helped me get it straightened out – and made sure since it was the court's mistake I wasn't charged with a failure to appear.

But then the next notice I received had the same

mistake. And the next one after that. It went on for so long it became a joke to us. So much time passed the charges ended up being dropped because all the witnesses died from overdoses or lost their minds from the meth.

But by then Roz and I had become friends. I started supplying her with the copper wire she needed for her knitting project, which is how I got arrested again. Copper is so expensive there's a big demand for cheaper sources of it, and a lot of people strip copper from buildings and public fixtures to sell on the black market."

"So you were arrested for selling bootlegged copper wire?"

"No, I was arrested for pot; on my way back from picking up a supply of copper wire."

"I hate to break up story hour, but our tail seems to have picked up a tail. And it looks military."

"Good. It's about time the military got involved." Dick Cheney sounded almost too cheerful. Fung Wah was beginning to suspect all three brothers had gotten a little too deeply in character, and blamed himself. He obviously hadn't done a very good job of explaining they were only using common American names, not their personality disorders.

By the time they reached Camarillo there was a third vehicle tailing them, and it looked to Roz like it was some kind of van. And not a little sport utility van, but one of those big delivery vans. It made her wonder how many people would be coming to the party. She was also glad she'd driven the taco truck. As cramped at it would be it still held more people than her little Nissan did.

She was even more glad when her eyes adjusted to the dark in the unlit driveway of the Pleasant Valley Sunday Rehabilitation and Psychiatric Treatment Center and she saw how many more people would be getting in.

At first the treatment center seemed deserted because there wasn't a single light on. But when Blade opened the back door and whistled, it was perfectly obvious it wasn't deserted. It had just been abandoned by a large number of their patients. And all of them were now getting in the back of the taco truck.

"Hurry up! We're being tailed and need to get out of here." She spoke in a whispered shout she really didn't need to use because it appeared nobody in the center would hear even if she shouted at the top of her lungs.

Roz had managed to shake the three vehicles following her when she got onto the 101 at Rice and immediately back off again at Rose. She then wound her way through the back roads east of the 101 until connecting with the one she hoped would take her to the treatment center.

While the fact there had been two cars and a

van tailing her did come as a bit of a surprise, what really floored her was when the last person to step out of the shadows got into the taco truck. It was the Void. And she was carrying a mop handle. So were three of the other mental patients.

"You're late." Constance slammed the door behind her. "The smoke signals said you'd be here at one AM so we've been waiting since half past twelve. We almost lost someone who actually realized for the first time he's afraid of the dark. It was a breakthrough for him though, since it means he's afraid of something other than people." Carlos started to introduce himself but Constance kept talking.

"Jerry took a chance and went back in to call for a cab when we thought nobody was coming, but only got what he swears sounds like the menu Comcast customers get when they try calling customer service. He says any number he dialed routed him to the same pointless menu that never takes anyone anywhere."

When Roz heard the first bullet shriek as it tore through the rear door of the taco truck, she heard another voice she recognized.

"Not again!" Suzanne Shill screamed, diving for the floor. "Look, if you want to get us out of this alive you'd better let Constance drive. But don't listen to her when she calls you a bitch. It's just her delusion talking."

A blinding light appeared in the rear view mirror

as the Void plopped herself in Roz's lap and told her to get the hell out from under her as the van's wheels announced their departure from the driveway with a loud squeal.

Roz wasn't sure how, but all three vehicles pursuing them had caught up, and at least one person was shooting at them. They must have been government because their car had a searchlight.

Sunday had begun in Camarillo with Constance Void behind the wheel yet again while being shot at in a high speed chase. As far as Smokey was concerned, it was just another Pleasant Valley Sunday.

CHAPTER NINETEEN

Toole didn't know why, but Roz had picked up the same Rastafarian he'd seen in Venice the day before. And it was possible two of the five Chinamen she'd picked up at Point Mugu State Park were from the Krispy Kreme parking lot surveillance video. But that made no sense. Nor did the fact that Roz was driving a taco truck.

Just how much room is there for passengers in a taco truck?

To make matters worse, not long after following them back onto PCH heading north, he picked up a tail. The vehicle looked government to him, most likely military and he presumed it was the admiral and his driver. Who else would it be this close to the Mugu Air Naval Base? But it looked like they had another couple of passengers in the car, which led Toole to wonder if the admiral and his driver were double agents and the passengers in the back seat were their Mossad handlers.

More and more he was convinced there was something big going down in Ventura County. First the feed on the treatment center's data stream was cut, then he found the curious recording on the clinic's phone line when he intercepted it hoping someone would place a call. He almost got sidetracked in a search to see if Comcast was owned by the Israelis, but decided to put that on a back burner and look it up later.

Also he was pretty sure there was a large van behind the admiral's car that was also tailing him, because it didn't make sense that it would be following the admiral. Unless of course it was some of the admiral's pot smoking friends, like those from a certain high school in Pasadena as fond of moonlight drives along the Pacific coast as they were of plotting to detonate bombs at graduation parties. It didn't occur to him they were possibly on their way to meet up with a carload of MILFs listening to Jack Johnson.

When he followed Roz up Rice Avenue and onto the 101 going southbound and watched her take evasive action by quickly taking the next exit at Rose, it made him realize something he hadn't expected. Not only could she handle a taco truck like a boss, but his girl had more going on for her than just a pretty face and a figure that filled out her bailiff uniform with all the right curves in all the right places. And it was making Little Toole stand at attention in a way he hadn't anticipated, considering it wasn't customary for Little Tooles to stand at attention for bailiffs. Not where he was from, anyway.

Though he wasn't quite sure why she was doing it, there was no question in Toole's mind Roz was undoubtedly going to the Pleasant Valley Sunday Rehabilitation and Psychiatric Treatment Center in Camarillo to get Constance Void and the data stored in her brain to safety. Perhaps it was a part of the bailiff's job description people never knew about. What he did know was he wanted to make sure she succeeded at that job. If for no other reason than to watch those curves do what they do so well.

With that in mind, Toole amused himself by leading the admiral and his friends behind him on a wild goose chase up the Conejo Grade. The seven percent incline was steep enough to slow down the van behind the admiral, which proved only that it wasn't a van load of high school boys looking for MILFs along Pacific Coast Highway to smoke pot with in the full moon.

When gradually the admiral's car and the Scooby

Mystery Van fell behind and he hadn't seen either for almost a full minute, he turned around at the Thousand Oaks exit and headed back down the 101 into Pleasant Valley. The lights at night descending into the valley reminded him of the Christmas trees his mother refused to ever have anything to do with.

It also reminded him of suburban pastimes like kids' soccer leagues and Sunday barbecues, two other things she refused to have anything to do with. She said it was because soccer moms are bitches and barbecues are entirely too predictable, just like soccer moms.

He realized the drive down PCH and back following Roz had taken longer than he'd expected and it was well past midnight Sunday already. As he took the exit for Camarillo, he checked his rear view mirror, hoping he'd lost his tail. Both of them. And at first it looked like he had. He took a brief detour to see that Suzanne Shill's car was still in the Ralph's parking lot, then headed for the treatment center.

Toole turned out his lights as he approached, hoping Roz wouldn't notice his car idling on the side street. It was impossible to make out who was who as a string of people stepped out of the shadows carrying what looked like single use plastic grocery bags with something in them. It made no sense. Weren't single use plastic grocery bags banned in Ventura County?

Maybe they made a special exception for mental patients. One of them seemed to be carrying a small rug, which also made no sense.

They all got into the van, and he was pretty sure the last one was Constance Void. Not because of anything she did that distinguished her from the rest of the shadows, but because he recognized the red Chuck Taylors winking at him in the moonlight. They were exactly the right footwear for the great escape from that mental midget with his dangerously sharp object.

He also recognized someone behind her in a lab coat, and the only other figure that looked like a woman had hair that made him think of Medusa. There had to be at least six or maybe even seven people in all who got into the back of the taco truck. Once again Toole found himself wondering just how much room there is in those things. And then he wondered whether he could get away with asking for single use plastic bags at the market by pretending to hear voices.

He was also puzzling over the four mop handles he counted going into the van. None of them had mop heads. *How is anyone supposed to mop without a mop head?* But he was abruptly distracted from thoughts of mop heads and single use plastic bags when he heard the first shot at the exact same time a floodlight lit up the taco truck from behind him.

The admiral and Team Mossad had caught up with him, and he could only hope his girl would let

Constance Void take the wheel. He'd been schooled on what the Void can do in a high speed chase, and as much as he and Little Toole liked watching Roz at the wheel, he would rather she make it through the ordeal unscathed so he and Little Toole can show her just how much it meant to him.

Under a hail of gunfire the taco truck took off, lumbering up the driveway's steep incline before sending a shower of sparks flying when the rear end scraped the pavement as the street leveled out at the top and they shot down Las Posas Boulevard. The taco truck sped down the street into the night with the other two vehicles in close pursuit.

To his surprise, Toole found himself bringing up the rear. Wishing he'd been issued a weapon by the NSA, he imagined his supervisor patiently explaining to him the NSA doesn't issue guns to its employees because there are no field agents in the NSA. But his supervisor was wrong. Not only was Toole a field agent, he was a stellar field agent.

He was also fairly certain he knew where Constance was going, and because of that he decided to make a bold move. If he didn't do something to slow down the admiral and Team Mossad, his girls wouldn't be able to outrun them.

The stellar field agent sped through a side street in the sleeping suburb in order to get ahead of the admiral. Just after the speeding taco truck flew past the dark street where he sat waiting, Toole pulled out onto Pleasant Valley Road right in front of the admiral's oncoming car.

How many times had Toole seen the writers of some television show resort to the T-Bone as a cheap escape from a tight spot in the action sequence rather than employ some actual creativity? And it was always when the central character finally relaxed, thinking he or she had gotten away from the drug lord serial killer evil government double agent. It was then they were slammed into in a merciless side impact in what was no longer a classic T-Bone, but a tired production device. The central character was so caught up in congratulating himself he never saw it coming. But the audience did. And it always bought the producers another fifteen minutes of airtime, which their advertisers loved.

And it was because they never saw it coming and because the admiral was an evil government double agent and because Toole needed to buy Constance Void and his Roz the time they desperately needed to reach their destination safely that Toole knew his twist on the old T-Bone production device would work.

He could have sworn he made eye contact with the admiral's surprised driver as his speeding car slammed into Toole's. And Toole could easily have been rendered unconscious and dragged from the car and tied up in some abandoned cellar for an unnecessary sequence where the evil government double agent explains everything to him, and also conveniently fills in all the plot holes.

But Toole was driving a Chrysler. Chryslers are gas guzzlers for a reason. All that weight from the solid steel frame and heavy duty body can withstand almost any impact. Especially the Sebring. Not only was he not rendered unconscious when the admiral's car T-Boned it, but he didn't even feel the impact when the van behind him slammed into the rear end of the admiral's car, making a messy Mossad sandwich of the corrupt admiral and his passengers on Pleasant Valley Road. In fact, the Chrysler's engine didn't even stall out.

Toole left Mossad to clean up his mess as he pulled away and headed for Oxnard to the place his finely tuned instincts told him Constance Void was going. As he took the incline up the freeway ramp, he noticed something rattling around in the trunk and wondered what the T-Bone had knocked loose back there. But he had plenty of time to find out once he got to where he was going.

Right now, Roz and Constance Void needed him. They might think they were in safe hands, but little did they know what those Chinamen who were in the taco truck with them were up to. And if his hunch was right, there would be more waiting for them when they reached their destination.

The mysterious clunking in the trunk grew louder as he mashed the gas pedal to the floor and tried to make up for lost time, determined to think of a way to get his girl and the Void out of the situation safely.

CHAPTER TWENTY

The GWEN tower in south Oxnard sits at the very
edge of an agricultural field that's planted with
strawberries early each spring in advance of the world
famous California Strawberry Festival. Held in Oxnard
every year on the third weekend in May, most locals
avoid it, and one only has to see the traffic and
astronomical parking fees to know why. Although it
had been harvested for the festival, the next crop
wasn't far behind.

Still green and thirsty, the berries had just been
watered. As Constance Void led the others toward the
tower they found themselves soaked to the knees in not
just irrigation water, but the caustic agricultural
chemicals the berries are routinely sprayed with. The

volatile mixture made it entirely unpleasant. In fact, it stung. A lot.

Carlos Castaneda was discovering something else to be afraid of and congratulating himself on his recovery from xenophobia because of it. He had just started asking Constance Void why Flocks News didn't tell people to be afraid of all the chemicals sprayed on their food, but was interrupted by a loud rattling noise accompanying the headlights rapidly approaching the field. The Void was relieved, since the last thing Jerry needed was to overhear a discussion that could give him a reason to be afraid of food.

"That's Creepy Guy with the leaf blowers. Which means the others can't be too far behind, so let's get moving."

Toole couldn't take the mystery noise any longer. As soon as he got to the edge of the field he jumped from the car and yanked open the trunk to see what had been banging around back there. Inside were two innocent looking leaf blowers pretending to be minding their own business. And he had no idea why.

It made about as much sense as the four mop handles he'd counted going into Roz's taco truck with the mental patients in Camarillo. Nor did he have any idea why he grabbed the leaf blowers before sprinting through the field toward the GWEN tower with one in each hand.

Had he been paying a little more attention to

what the Void had said during group therapy, he would have been spared the confusion. But the confusion had actually started in that group therapy when there was no therapy at all, so Toole is to be forgiven.

As soon as she saw Toole with the leaf blowers, Constance called out for the mop handles and duct tape, then nodded to the Rastafarian. Without a word, the lanky black man with dreadlocks set up his kettle drum and began playing as though he was some kind of military drummer or perhaps a fifer marching soldiers into war. Only with a Reggae beat.

Constance took one of the leaf blowers and Jack Kerouac took the other. Toole watched in utter fascination as they dropped chocolate pudding in a cup down each chute. Next they duct taped two mop handles horizontally across the end of each chute, being sure to leave ample room for the pudding to squeeze between the mop handles.

Once satisfied the mop handles were securely in place with the duct tape, the Void called out for the toilet paper. Toole pictured an Army sergeant calling for his artillery gunman to load more ammunition. Glenn, Jerry, Carlos and Haj each pulled four rolls out from the bags they'd had slung over their shoulders all night and handed them ceremoniously to the Void and Jack Kerouac, who slid them over the mop handles. Toole looked at Roz hoping she'd know what was about to happen, but she was even more in the dark than he was.

At least he knew this was the GWEN tower that had been defaced once before with chocolate pudding and toilet paper. Not only did she have no idea what any of this was about, she was still puzzling over why she was compelled to bring all that pudding.

Toole looked around nervously for midgets or any sign of the admiral and Team Mossad, and hoped the Void was ready to do whatever it was she was preparing to do. He'd been so caught up in her preparation of the leaf blowers he'd completely forgotten about the threat the Chinamen from the Krispy Kreme posed to Constance.

But rather than lurk menacingly, Toole saw the four of them, including the two he was most concerned about, had positioned themselves around the base of the tower facing outward – one at the north corner, one at the south, one at the east and one at the west. They had apparently become sentries guarding the tower from anything that might blow in from one of the four corners of the world. Only sentries whose job description included sitting in the lotus position and meditating.

He watched as the mental patient he'd seen with what had looked like a rug walked toward the Chinamen and spread what turned out to actually be a rug on the ground next to the one facing west. When

Toole saw him take up a fistful of sandy soil, rub it between both palms and then let it fall from his hands, he realized the man must be Haj. And he was joining the Chinamen to do his Isha salat, the prayer performed customarily between dusk and dawn by devout Muslims.

He knelt and began reciting the first sura of the Quran. Toole had heard the mental patients discuss how it would take their collective efforts to reverse the curse, and wondered if this had anything to do with that.

The gentle Muslim teacher of culinary arts hadn't wanted to draw attention away from more pressing things, but he had not heard the voices since shortly after he got into the taco truck at Point Mugu State Park.

It was the first time in years he hadn't been tormented by them. He wasn't sure if it was because of the colorful knit cap he'd been asked to put on when he got into the truck or if the magic Constance Void was making had already started working to stop the shenanigans and reverse the curse put on him years ago. Either way, he considered this to be the most important salat of his life as he gave thanks to his god between tears of joyful gratitude.

"Okay, now comes the hard part." Constance turned to Suzanne and Roz and handed them the leaf blowers. "Ladies, I need you to take these so the others can have their hands free for climbing the tower."

She showed them how to start the leaf blowers but warned them to wait until her signal. Toole could see the confusion on Roz's face, but all the others seemed to know exactly what was going on. Especially Suzanne Shill, who seemed to have been transformed.

He watched as the rest of the Pleasant Valley Sunday patients began to climb the tower in silence, the only sound being the kettle drum softly playing beneath the Rastafarian's remarkably long slender hands.

"A little higher, Carlos. You need to get above the part my incantation is directed at, so go up another twenty feet at least."

Carlos Castaneda was enjoying discovering yet another thing he was afraid of more than himself and people who were different. The higher he climbed up the tower the more terrified he got, and he was loving it. Until he started worrying about possibly developing a fear of climbing back down.

He had just asked himself what he would do if he had to take a leak when he noticed Glenn had stopped climbing and started pointing. Constance had insisted Glenn be the first to climb up the tower and position herself as high as possible so the superhero could do what she does best.

"She's pointing," Carlos called down. The faint glow of a single headlight approached the field. With it was the shrieking rattle that one often hears when a badly leaking transmission low on fluid gets into an argument with a loose fan belt over who started it when everybody knows it was the cracked radiator.

"According to the Department of Transportation cameras, a banged up white delivery van missing both of its front hubcaps and dragging its bumper got off the freeway at Rice Avenue trailing a thick cloud of oily smoke five minutes ago."

Jerry had positioned himself at the lowest spot on the tower he could manage after climbing above the pudding zone. He needed to be seated comfortably so he could focus on accessing his wireless connection and keeping them posted on any pertinent updates he could get data on.

Constance turned to Roz and Suzanne and told them to spread their legs for support, bend their knees slightly and brace themselves for the kick. Suzanne had inexplicably smeared strawberry juice from what must have been the only ripe berry in the field on her cheeks and forehead.

The Void couldn't decide if she looked more like a steampunk Chumash warrior in a lab coat or one of the lost tribes of Ghostbusters. Raising her right arm above her head she told them to start the leaf blowers and to fire when she dropped it.

"One."

"Two."

"Three."

"FIRE!" The Void shouted as she dropped her arm like the flag girl at a drag race in small town America where drag racing down Main Street is all there is to do on a Saturday night.

Unless of course one wants to go home and get rid of all their old calendars so they have room for one from this century, since drag racing hasn't been done in small town America since date raping the flag girl and doing meth became the favorite pastimes.

Constance began reciting the incantation as the licensed marriage and family therapist turned warrior and the Ventura County Superior Court Bailiff unloaded eight rolls each of twin ply toilet paper and twenty four cups of chocolate pudding all over the Chinese and Israeli controlled base of South Oxnard's GWEN tower.

Illuminated by the drive-in movie moon above them, Constance Void called out the words she'd been given in her dream as the Rastafarian kept the Reggae beat and Glenn Greenworld pointed fearlessly at the approaching mangled van with one working headlight.

Meanwhile, Toole did his best to ready himself for the unavoidable confrontation he knew was about to go down.

Blade, on the other hand, wanted to know more about this wireless connection Constance Void kept mentioning. The hacker felt helpless without a screen to look at, and toyed with the idea of climbing up next to Jerry so he could read over his shoulder. In the end, he lay down between two rows of berries on his belly and watched the toilet paper and pudding fly as the Void recited the strangest incantation he'd ever heard. Not that he'd heard many.

"May the most unexpected of all alliances form out of the dirt of these fields and shove pudding up your shiny things. You can run and you can hide, but you can never stop them. They will always find you and your shenanigans. No matter where you go or what you do, they will be watching. And they will always have pudding. Never forget, to become enamored of one's powers is to lose them. At once."

The incantation and the chocolate toilet paper redecorating of the tower base took less than forty seconds, but by the time both were completed, the van had driven right into the field. Well, actually it lumbered. Or maybe it was more like a lurch and shudder and hiss.

Either way, the first shots rang out as Constance was saying the last line of the incantation. The Void was not at all bothered by it, though. Perhaps because they had already been shot at that night and she had grown inured to the sound of gunfire over the past few days. Or perhaps it was simply because she was from Oxnard.

Toole on the other hand was deeply bothered by it.

And so was Roz. As much as she might want to believe in magic at that very moment, she wasn't sure she could believe chocolate pudding could make them impervious to bullets. But not Suzanne. She was beginning to suspect it could defend against many things, possibly even bullets.

Speaking of bullets, Suzanne wanted more ammunition for the leaf blowers because she was just getting started. Improvising, she began picking green strawberries and dropping them down the chute of her leaf blower.

Midway up the tower, Jack Kerouac balanced himself and took careful notes, certain he had a bestseller on his hands. Of course in his version, the evil doers would be a private security firm and their buddies in the CIA, but the writer was confident he could work the facts he had into his completely fictional story expertly.

He was also confident he would never touch another drop of alcohol as long as he lived. Which might not be much longer, because unless he was mistaken, an entire street gang had just poured out of the van that just arrived. As soon as their feet hit the ground every one of them started shooting without a single hesitation. And like most street gangs, it really didn't seem to matter to any of them just who they hit.

Of course Toole suspected it had something to do with the Israelis, because not only did the admiral and his driver get out of the Scooby Van with them, but the woman from the restaurant, the one with Jewish hair, and the man in the red yarmulke from Venice were with him.

He kicked himself for not following the man in the red yarmulke that day, and also for not stabbing the woman in the thorax with his spoon when he'd first thought of it at Canter's. Welcome to the jungle, indeed.

It was Roz who identified them by their curious coupling of fine Italian leather jackets with cheaply made poor quality shoes. There's only one kind of man whose character is that questionable: a poser.

"It's the Poser Gang. That's not good. Not at all."

Always the officer of the court, Roz was up on her criminal gangs. "They're mercenary gang bangers – in it for the money only. They say those fighting for their ideals are the most dangerous of all fighters, and the Posers are no exception. They worship money, and contract out to the highest bidder."

"Posers?" Suzanne seemed confused, though it was hard to tell if it was because of their name or their perfectly accessorized outfits which seemed to have come straight out of Abercrombie and Fitch.

"They're from Orange County."

It came as no surprise to anyone the only place mercenary gangsters like the Posers could be from is Orange County.

Because of how corrupt both law enforcement and prosecutors are there, the natural byproduct is sons who are in it for as much personal gain as their fathers are. Proving once again the line between legal and illegal is often up to who's interpreting it and what their motivation is. And their credentials, of course.

The Posers are free to openly advertise their services, quite literally posting signs on the lawns of their respectable split levels with attached two car garage and Hummer in the driveway. In fact, their business card could be found in the wallet of most staff members at the county prosecutor's office. This sort of thing tends to be the case in counties plagued with corrupt judicial systems. Constance Void blames the robes.

At that moment, Blade knew their presence meant word of the reappearance of the Wu had not just gotten out, it had spread. The Wu was the last person those who control the lucrative illicit global drug market wanted competition from.

As the Wu imparts the ancient wisdom that allows a person to control their own state of consciousness as they see fit, naturally – without taking any chemical substance at all – demand for those products will plummet. The CIA was not likely to put up with that. Nor was Mossad, as far as Toole could see. Where do you think Mossad and the CIA get their extra pocket change for those pesky unforeseen expenses, like supplying guns to terrorists and guerrilla soldiers?

After all, weren't both Mossad and the CIA really nothing more than the secret police of capitalism?

Blade had seen chatter on the back channels about the CIA and Mossad working together in the States with a third party on something big, and had a hunch he might know what was behind the mercenaries' presence there. Considering who that third party was, it made perfect sense to him that particular alliance would be contracting the Poser Gang. The corporate elite's method of expanding their market had been successful for so long it practically had its own trademark.

"Basically, both the CIA and Mossad are partners on the same dance floor. It's the particular third party behind these mercenaries here that I find telling."

"The third party? Who are they?" Smokey appeared to be surprisingly adept at multi-tasking as he listened to Blade while pulling his own piece out from his jeans and returning fire.

"Walmart. Plunge a country into poverty along with the self-degradation that results from saturating it with the CIA's drugs and people will do anything – including work in a sweat shop for next-to-nothing. Those who don't want to do that can always sell an organ to Mossad's organ traffickers."

"So Walmart, the CIA and Mossad went in together on the Poser Gang's fees to make sure Constance Void here doesn't cut into the profits of their joint corporate cartel? Are the American people aware of any of this?"

Blade couldn't answer the question. In fact, no one could, but only because they were too busy trying to figure out how the sweet gentle boy with the smoke colored eyes from Port Hueneme got his hands on a nine millimeter. Especially Suzanne, who was beginning to wonder if the Oxnard Police simply let everybody they arrest keep their fireworks and weapons to cut down on paperwork. But more than that, she was wondering if he had an extra one she could use.

Had Carlos not been up on the GWEN tower, he would have elaborated on what Blade was trying to say, the way only an anthropologist could. He would have told them when the CIA and Mossad come in with all their shenanigans to a Kosovo or a Honduras or a Guatemala, the true target is memory.

Nobody knew better than Carlos the hazards that spring up from losing one's memory. Disrupting the memory of the individual is one thing, but blocking the collective memory of an entire people is another thing entirely. It's pay dirt. It's the easiest way to exploit them.

Collective amnesia is the most direct route to

oppression. The society that fails to remember how oppression has historically worked is the easiest society to oppress. They never see it coming. With that, you've got everything you want. Because history forgotten is history repeated for profit.

He then would have explained the way it's done. The steps are always the same. First you have your corporate partners send in the missionaries they support to get people wanting to emulate them, dress like them, live like them, worship like them. But basically what those witless missionaries have done is teach them how to worship wealth. With the worship of wealth comes the discontentment of knowing you have no way to attain that wealth.

Then Carlos would have quoted something from one of his favorite anthologies: "Desire is the origin of bitterness." The people the missionaries have come to "save" get so caught up in desire and bitterness they forget who they are. Then it's merely a matter of liberally applying some shenanigans with the help of the intelligence community until there's justification to send in the military because chaos. Works like a charm. Every time.

Follow the simple steps and you've got fertile ground for the CIA's drugs, the mob's organ harvesters, the global pedophile's sex trafficking ring and Walmart's sweat shops. Chaos accomplished, and all that wealth gained from it gets funneled upward in an increasingly narrow channel.

But Carlos was up on the tower, so all he could do was hope he had the opportunity later to explain everything.

Suzanne, on the other hand, was thinking about drugs. It surprised her how much more clearly she was thinking without all that Ambien she'd been taking. For the first time ever she had to admit to herself there really was no difference between it and the devil weed Constance Void used: a drug is a drug.

She was about to ask Blade how involved Mossad and the CIA are with the pharmaceutical industry, when she realized they were surrounded. The Poser's bullets had begun to fly from all directions. Diving between two rows of strawberries, she found herself right next to Blade wondering if she would ever get the opportunity to ask him. It was starting to look hopeless for all of them.

No sooner had the mercenary street gang surrounded them than the field lit up with the unmistakable bouncing headlights of the Oxnard thuggie in his low rider with hydraulics.

The bass booming through their rear mounted speakers had begun vibrating the GWEN tower. What seemed like it might be a handful of gang bangers in a half dozen low riders turned out to be dozens as Colonia Chiques defied the gang injunction by showing up to represent. In no time at all they had assessed the situation and started returning fire to the invading gang.

Just before Las Colonias made their music blasting hydraulic entrance Toole had thought he heard a deep, low humming along with a peculiar percussion coming from the direction of Fung Wah and his nephews.

He'd dismissed it, thinking it was one of those Mongolian throat singing things guys like that do when they're faced with certain death and coping with it by meditating. But after Las Colonias cut the music and got out of their lowriders, he was certain he could hear it. Only it was coming from above.

"She's pointing again," Carlos shouted. "Only this time she's pointing up at the sky."

Toole, Roz and Suzanne looked upward just as it registered they were also feeling a sudden wind. Had they not all been in mortal danger, it would have been a good time to make a humorous connection between that wind and Fung Wah. But they were in fact very much in mortal danger, and sadly the opportunity to break the tension with humor about breaking wind was lost.

Glenn continued to point at the darkness and the others secretly hoped this would be one of the times when her superpower vanquished the oncoming evil.

But the universe had other plans and the only

one who might know why is Bill Nye, but he refuses to say.

Without a sound, black ropes dropped from four stealth helicopters and what looked to Toole like a bunch of Buddhist monks in robes dropped to the ground. Only, since when do Buddhist monks have swords strapped to their backs?

"Shaolin monks, and they've got their blades," Blade said, not even remotely amused by the irony. "There's only one reason the most dangerous assassins in the history of China are here. Nobody is going to make it out of this alive."

It was at that point Toole realized he'd been dead wrong about the monks only coming to visit the Los Angeles Dharma Center to play with sand. It appears they were more interested in playing with blades. The Dharma Center should have been the first place he visited instead of Venice Beach with its almost naked breathing people. And that amateur mistake was about to cost all of them their lives.

"Fuck that shit," Roz said, startling Toole. Although he had to admit, Little Toole liked it when his girl talked dirty.

"Being an officer of the court doesn't come without its perks." She pulled her smart phone from her pocket so fiercely it looked lethal. Little Toole almost fainted.

As the monks advanced on them, seemingly

focused on Constance Void and the Fung Wah boys, Toole did his best to block Roz from danger with his body, although he was pretty certain one of those monks' blades would cut through him like butter and slice and dice anyone standing behind him.

But the truth is, it comforted him to think he was doing something useful, even if he was not, so try not to judge. Most of us would have done the same thing in his position.

Suzanne on the other hand had loaded both leaf blowers with green strawberries and aimed them at the approaching Shaolin monks. She was about to fire when out of the corner of her eye she noticed movement.

"What is that moving out there?"

She said it just as Carlos called down that Glenn was pointing at something out in the field. It was too dark to see anything but shadows, but those shadows were moving.

At first it seemed to all of them that it was a bunch of children, which was the last thing any of them needed. Children really shouldn't be around loaded weapons. Or blades. Especially at night. In Oxnard. It was all Toole could do to worry about protecting Roz and Little Toole without having to worry about a bunch of kidlets. But Constance knew exactly who it was.

"Fuck me six ways from Sunday." She said it

under her breath, but it was loud enough for Little
Toole to hear. Toole immediately wished it hadn't been.
   "It's the midgets."
   The sixteen badly behaved Jewish midgets had
arrived, and they had it out for the monks. And the
reason they had it out for the monks wouldn't surprise
anyone. When they got close enough for Constance to
see the freshly sharpened Izmail in each midget's hand,
she looked at the monks' robes and knew this was
going to be one bloody battle.
   Roz had taken it upon herself to call for
reinforcements. To be precise, she didn't actually call.
She text messaged. They tend to get quicker results
than calls do.
       As the bloodbath between the midgets and the
Shaolin monks began, it started to look like the
mercenary gang bangers out of the OC were having
chopped liver for dinner and Las Colonias were the
unwilling donors. But not like the liver Portnoy spent
two hundred and eighty nine pages complaining about.
Oxnard thuggies don't go for that kind of kink. That
shit's too nasty even for Colonia gangsters.
   Roz's text message had gotten through loud and
clear. Largely because El Sud had their text alert turned
on full volume. Another set of bouncing headlights and
loud bass blasting through trunk mounted speakers
announced the arrival of El Sud, better known by
Oxnard Gang Enforcement as The Southside, in their

own lowriders on hydraulics.

The two bitterly rival gangs were both violating the gang injunction that night, but not to fight each other. There was no way they were going to let a bunch of capitalist wannabe gangsters come into THEIR territory, especially the ones being paid by Walmart.

"Thiz MY house!"

That was the battle cry that night as they stood shoulder to shoulder and fought against the deadliest assassins in the history of China and the most well outfitted thuggies this side of Abercrombie and Fitch. And the most vicious midgets any of them had ever seen. But that goes without saying.

Constance Void was relieved none of them wore wide cut board shorts that night, but Toole was concerned about the risks of possible back door entry through the exposed cracks peeking out from the waistband of their fashionably color coordinated underwear.

Speaking of color coordinated, he turned to see Suzanne Shill unload both barrels of green strawberries from the almost-lethal leaf blowers.

"Bring it on, bitches!" She was aiming at the Posers mostly, although more than one midget got a black eye that night.

While the official story would remain for decades to come that the two gangs worked in solidarity out of an allegiance to their city, the allegiance was far deeper and much more personal for every one of them.

Each thuggie that fought and bled in what became known as Oxnard's infamous Battle of Strawberry Fields had lost at least one family member to Israeli illegal organ traffickers operating in Central America.

The lucky ones died quickly. The unfortunate ones lingered in excruciating misery for years after, so badly disabled from the careless harvesting of their kidney they spent the rest of their lives unable to work or do anything useful for their families. What's more, the money they were offered for their kidney was often not even paid, or if it was, they only received a fraction of what had been promised.

And most of them had mothers, aunties or sisters working at Walmart. Watching them try to make ends meet with dignity while living on minimum wage for jobs that would never schedule them enough hours to be full time had driven them all to a deep hatred of the company and the heartless bitch legal counsel who helped them establish their employment policies.

Those policies had allowed the company to suck the life out of the communities it blighted with its stores, since the majority of its employees had to go on food stamps and medical assistance to get by. Which – of course – the community, not Walmart, paid for.

As for the CIA, each and every one of those Oxnard thuggies was well aware that if it hadn't been for the Agency things in Honduras wouldn't have reached a point of such critical mass their relatives had to sell their organs to survive.

And lastly, but not least, was the fact that this very field had been worked by friends, relations and the extended family of every Oxnard thuggie, and nobody disrespects the territory of the hardest working people in America. Nobody had more right to declare "Thiz MY house" than the Mexican immigrants whose blood had done the actual work of farming it.

Sorting out just exactly what brought such a vicious gang of freelance mercenaries and the Chinese assassins to Oxnard Plains that night was something that would be poorly understood and misinterpreted by scholars for years to come, as well. And let's not even get started on how badly Flocks News mangled the story.

But what it started with was turf. Fed up with the Israelis monopolizing the illegal organ harvesting market in New York City, the Chinese headed west for sandier pastures and set up shop in Los Angeles.

Of course, the Israeli organ traffickers were not happy with how lucrative the change of scenery had been for their Chinese friends. At first they kept a respectful distance, staying on the down low with their activities when they moved to L.A. and discovered that there was just as much poverty-stricken desperation there as in New York.

But when word started to circulate that the Wu of prophecy walked among them again after centuries, all of that changed.

The awakening of the most powerful metaphysical figure in history started a race between them to be the first one to take possession of the Wu.

Each side knew it was imperative to stop her from teaching others the knowledge she'd brought with her. How would they be able to dominate anyone if people learned how to alter their brain waves, access their own memories, think for themselves and connect with others?

Only the Chinese hoped to take her alive though, planning to reverse engineer her natural abilities and create a synthetic version. Walmart, on the other hand, along with the CIA and Mossad just wanted her dead. But isn't that pretty much how psychopathic corporations and the intelligence industries they own are with anyone who threatens their God-given right to profit off of human suffering?

At the very heart of it, that night's battle was a rivalry between the combined efforts of the CIA, the Walmart Corporation and Mossad versus China's Ministry of State Secrets.

And the sixteen badly behaved Jewish midgets showed up after intercepting some smoke signals just because they like to kick ass. With sharp knives and uncircumcised men. They have no alliances with anyone except each other.

What both Chinese intelligence and the corporate owned psychopaths failed to take into consideration was what might happen if the sixteen badly behaved Jewish midgets heard about the fight and showed up that night.

Of course, Toole knew better than anyone else there that night the battle was primarily about the sovereignty of the human mind. What the Wu had brought to teach was a way to ensure each person retains that sovereignty, and the global corporate cartel running the show was not willing to let that happen.

Enslaving the human mind with drugs, religion, technology and fear were far too profitable. And that profit was something they were willing to kill for.

It was a battle that would be the envy of anyone who worked on the 2002 production of Gangs of New York. Oblivious to the larger battle being waged between the forces of good and evil beyond that strawberry field, thuggies from rival Oxnard street gangs shot it out with thuggies from the corporate boardroom while the larger war between forces that influenced all of them fought it out for control of that influence.

And valiant as the Oxnard gangsters might be, it seemed they were running out of either ammunition or energy, or possibly both.

Bloodied Hispanic boys lay on the ground on one

side of a row of strawberries and mortally wounded mercenaries lay on the other, their blood staining the green unripe berries an unnatural red, a red that was obviously not plant-based.

It was one of those things vegan conspiracy theorists would speculate about at length on the internet, and continue to bring up for years to come. Row after row was the same. As far as the eye could see, it was bloody strawberry fields forever.

And the losses were even worse for the men in robes. Blade was certain the reputation of Shaolin monks had suffered irreversible damage that night. Not a single midget had so much as a scratch on him, unless you count the black eyes. But there was a pile of bloody Shaolin foreskin Toole didn't want to even think about near the tower. Yet despite not wanting to think about it, he found himself wondering just why the midgets piled them so close to all that pudding.

Certain his team still had the advantage, Admiral Thomas Thumbsen, his driver, the woman with Jewish hair and an intact thorax, and the man from Venice in the red yarmulke stepped out from the safety of the shadows where they'd been cowering. Pointing their guns at Toole and the two women, the admiral claimed victory only the way an American military leader can after everybody else has done the work of fighting the battle for him.

While Constance couldn't see her doing it, she

could feel Glenn had aimed her finger directly at the admiral and pointed with all her might.

"On the ground, you three. And you up there, come down. Now. Or I start shooting, starting with your friend from the NSA here."

"I don't think so." Constance didn't think anybody on the tower really cared whether the admiral shot the NSA agent or not, but kept that to herself.

"The night is young, and we're just getting started. Care for some pudding with your shenanigans?"

And with that, the sound of Reggae surrounded them all as kettle drums filled the air and an army of Rastafarians came from all directions.

Their drum straps were slung over their shoulders like the victors marching into a battle that's won before it's even begun so dismissed out of a need to do something more productive, like celebrate the random. Never in history has a Rastafarian army playing Reggae been vanquished, and it was no different this night.

"Call them off."

The admiral raised his pistol and held its shining silver barrel up against Constance Void's temple. She only smiled serenely.

"Go ahead and shoot."

So he did. As chocolate pudding squirted out of the barrel of his gun and ran down the side of her face, the Void giggled.

"No wonder you didn't want any pudding. You already had some, you rascal you!"

Still not clear on what had just happened, the admiral barked at his driver to shoot her. Constance just smiled and caught the chocolate pudding that shot out of the barrel of the driver's gun in her mouth with the expert skill of a trust fund baby at Donald Trump's frat house. Licking her lips coyly, she turned to the admiral once again.

"That all you got?"

Nodding to the man in the red yarmulke and the woman with Jewish hair, the two took aim with their matching his and her revolvers and fired chocolate pudding in twin streams that would have made James Joyce proud.

Jack Kerouac decided at that very moment he would call the central character in his novel Stephen Daedalus. He was certain he would take at least fourteen pages to describe the sound of the train whistle passing in the distance. Constance Void never would have the heart to tell him the trains stopped running hours earlier and what he had actually heard was the stellar wind of Agent Toole farting in relief that neither he nor his beloved Roz had been shot.

The man in the red yarmulke ran away like a school girl whose gun is possessed with the ghost of Bill Cosby's career. The Void was pretty certain that twin pudding stream was the kind of thing that would make the Ghostbusters proud. Weren't they always making dire warnings about what would happen if you crossed the streams? Since it was chocolate pudding and not protons shooting out of the revolvers, they were in no danger of anyone's molecules exploding at the speed of light. Only taste buds at the speed of chocolate.

The woman with Jewish hair didn't seem to like failure. She wasn't ready to give up. It was obvious from her evil grin she had something up her sleeve. Slowly she raised the walking cane Toole had seen leaning against the table they shared at Canter's. With the handle grasped in one hand and the other hand around the base of the cane, she pulled them apart and a steel blade that rivaled the work of the finest craftsman in Asia flashed in the moonlight.

In that same flash she charged toward the Void, building speed as she ran. Dread gripped Blade. Roz grabbed Toole's hand and squeezed as he realized he'd been wrong, Mossad didn't want the data in her head. They just wanted her dead. Or was it the Waltons? He'd lost track.

But Constance Void only yawned and wiped the pudding off her face with her fingertips. In a bad production of some third rate Samurai movie, the agent leaped into the air as she raised the sword high above her head.

But Glenn Greenworld had the Kidon assassin

in her sights, taking her eyes off the target only long enough to make brief eye contact with the Void and wink. Constance Void nodded her approval and Glenn focused with superhero intensity on the Samurai with Jewish hair.

As she did, the third rate Samurai movie mysteriously found enough in its production budget to film in slow motion. The assassin hung in mid-air long enough for Suzanne to realize it really is a good idea to wear a G-string with yoga pants because *damn girl those panty lines really are unsightly.*

It gave Constance Void enough time to calmly flick the chocolate pudding off her fingertips directly into the woman's face. As she reached striking distance, those looking on that night thought she was most certainly about to sever the Void's head from her body. Especially Blade, who knew the word for a Mossad assassin, Kidon, translated to "sharp end of the spear." He held his breath waiting for that sharp end to make its fatal blow. But that's not what happened. When the Kidon brought the sword down, all she had between her hands was three feet of toilet paper. Two ply toilet paper.

"Want some pudding to go with your shenanigans?"

Despite that defeat, the admiral refused to give up. He just kept shouting orders. Even as his Mossad assassin with the Jewish hair ran off into the night crying, toilet paper stuck to the bottom of her shoe. He wouldn't give up even as his driver abandoned him and ran after her. The admiral was absolutely certain the battle was going to turn around any minute now and his agenda would prevail. He just kept shouting pointless orders and refused to give up. If Bill O'Reilly hadn't been deep in meditation he would have approved.

Admiral Thumbsen even shouted pointlessly at the stealth choppers that landed in the strawberry field to load the Shaolin monks and get them the medical attention they obviously needed. He didn't care that they were too badly wounded to climb back up their ropes, or that when they got up there they wouldn't be able to sit down.

After all, helicopters don't routinely come equipped with rubber inflatable doughnuts. It didn't even matter to him that they weren't on the same side in this fight, he continued to bark orders at them anyway.

In his defense, it really isn't too hard to get that part confused. Not when you're economic bed partners and friends with both sides but in front of the cameras posing as adversaries and military foes of only one of those sides. It gets confusing.

So confusing in fact that he would have continued to bark pointless orders at the corporate mercenary gang bangers and the midgets too, but the freelance gang bangers were mostly mortally wounded and the midgets had joined the Rastafarians who were passing a blunt the size of his forearm between all of them.

One of the things the admiral failed to take into consideration that night was the reason the orders he shouted were pointless.

It was because there was only one Point there, and she was smiling down at him from the chocolate toilet paper covered GWEN tower.

Ignoring anything but the agony brought on by his own deflated ego, the admiral plopped himself down on top of a strawberry plant and began to cry, although later he insisted it was because a green strawberry the size of his fist went up his ass when he landed on it. All those chemicals sprayed on those berries couldn't have helped, either. They really do sting. A lot.

"How did this happen?" he wailed. While some might have considered it a rhetorical question, Constance Void couldn't resist the temptation to answer it.

"To become enamored of one's powers is to lose them. At once. Especially when your powers are used for shenanigans."

But Toole was fairly certain it was the smoke signals. How else would the Rastafarians have known to show up?

He, Roz and Suzanne helped the others on the ground eat a path through the chocolate pudding that coated the base of the tower so Glenn, Jerry, Carlos and Jack Kerouac could safely climb down without slipping, while Smokey and Pat Robertson kissed passionately. Not because bloodshed turned them on, but because they felt like it. And Bill O'Reilly and Dick Cheney were discovering they liked to watch. It turned them on almost as much as all the bloodshed.

Toole and Roz were turned on by it too. And so was Little Toole. In fact, they made a date to go see a Quentin Tarantino film together as soon as humanly possible. And Little Toole was definitely invited.

CHAPTER TWENTY ONE

Fung Wah was disappointed. He had never been to Oxnard and was really hoping to see the ox. But there were no oxen in Oxnard. None. Only bloody foreskin piled curiously close to the chocolate pudding that was dripping off the GWEN tower when he and the three nephews emerged from the powerful meditation that served to fortify the strength of the Wu's incantation.

Haj on the other hand didn't care whether he saw any oxen. He was just happy he wasn't hearing voices in his head and none of them were harmed while they were in meditation and prayer. It would be a while before Haj understood not only had none of them been harmed, but those prayers of his were essential to the level of protection they were all under.

By the time the Oxnard Police arrived at the Battle of Strawberry Fields, it was over. The first to retreat had been the admiral, but Toole wasn't too worried about Thumbsen getting away. The Poser's van didn't look like it would get him far. And he knew where the traitorous parasite lived.

Besides, Constance Void told him the Rastafarians would be taking care of it. If the Chinese didn't do it first.

Toole knew better than anyone how

disappointed the Israelis would be that the admiral wouldn't be getting that position as adviser to that Morgan Chase CEO after all. Their plans hinged on him seamlessly blending into the financial industry without attracting a lot of attention. Events of this night were sure to bring attention that even the CIA's media pets couldn't spin. He almost felt sorry for Flocks News.

All evidence either Las Colonias or El Sud had even been there was removed from the field. Which left only those freelancing corporate mercenaries to get their asses kicked by the Ventura County criminal justice system.

Forensics had a hard time determining what was blood and what was strawberry juice, and after a long study of evidence that made no sense to them concluded the peculiar street gang must have gotten into some kind of shootout with itself. Possibly over fashion correctness or some other issue involving the garment industry.

If it hadn't been for the legends that swirled up out of the dust of that field it might never have been known representatives of Oxnard's two most notoriously rival gangs were there that night. If it wasn't for the gossip that persisted, the solidarity between rival gangs and the courage with which they all represented might never have made it into the history books.

But stories like the Battle of Strawberry Fields don't die easily. While most blame the gang members themselves for bragging about it, those who were there know it was the midgets. Those bitches just can't pass up the opportunity to brag about their conquests.

As for the pile of foreskin, it has become a cold case. No one ever came forward to file a claim for missing foreskin, nor did anyone come forward to file a complaint about being forced to undergo a circumcision against his will.

As the sirens began to scream in the distance, Blade and Smokey helped load the last of the Oxnard gang bangers into their lowriders and promised to stay in touch.

The Rastafarians and the midgets were the first to leave after the cowardly admiral, but Constance Void had a feeling she'd be seeing them again.

All of the patients from Pleasant Valley Sunday climbed down from the GWEN tower and helped clean up the mess as best they could, except Jack Kerouac. He had climbed to the very top of the tower where there was a small platform sturdy enough for a man to stand, if he did so carefully.

To Constance it looked like a mizzen mast, which seemed odd because she wasn't one to linger on nautical terms. But perhaps it was because Jack Kerouac was standing with his arms spread wide shouting, "I'm on top of the world!"

Somewhere in the north Atlantic an iceberg is breaking loose with one mission in life: find Jack Kerouac and drown him before he sinks their lethal mission with the weight of his words. When men like Jack Kerouac have the kind of story to tell that he was writing, their words tend to be loaded. Constance was just happy it was his words that were loaded and not Jack Kerouac himself.

As she stood gazing at the writer lit up by the full moon spotlight above them, Fung Wah quietly spoke. It startled her somewhat because she hadn't heard him approach. She hadn't even known he'd come out of his meditative stupor.

"It is you who are climbing to the top of the world, Wu," he said cryptically.

"Wu who?"

"Wu who who?"

Constance realized this could go on forever, so decided to change her approach.

"Who are you calling Wu? And why?"

Constance Void worked quickly to remove the duct tape and free the mop handles from both leaf blowers as the wise elder explained what the Three had come down off Wu Mountain to do, and why. He told her how their grandfather had prepared the young men all their lives to bring the Wu, and how he had assisted when they arrived in California.

Knowing they would have many long hours for the details, he only gave her the Cliff notes, but it was enough for Constance to understand the meaning behind nautical terms working their way into her vocabulary recently.

She was about to cross an ocean and climb Wu Mountain in order to assume the position she had known all her life she was born into. She just didn't remember knowing it. Memory can be tricky like that. Especially when it comes to being reincarnated as the Wu.

If you were to ask an intelligence industry data analyst why the Wu didn't remember, he would first suspend disbelief, then tell you it's because memory is data. And data needs a storage device. Hardware. The brain is just that.

When the Wu was reborn, it was to a new storage device. It always takes time to download data from the cloud to a new device, no matter how confident the user is with their software. And if they've been misguided in the use of their operating system or it's been exposed to spyware or malware, it can seem almost impossible.

Just ask anyone who's switched from a Windows operating system to Linux. Or been raised by fundamentalists – especially if it's exposed them to televangelists for any length of time. Or for that matter, unduly influenced by men like Bill O'Reilly and his

342

friends.

Constance Void handed the old man a mop handle and smiled.

"Get to work, grasshopper."

As the two had been speaking, Constance noticed Roz and Suzanne open up the taco truck and watched with approval as Fung Wah's nephews rolled out the awning and set two folding tables with chairs out beneath it. Starting up the side lights and firing up the grill inside, they passed paper plates they'd hastily filled with whatever edibles they could get their hands on through the window to Toole and Glenn, who quickly sat at a table with them. Just as quickly, Roz handed Jerry and Haj two more plates and they sat at the other table.

As the screaming sirens pulled into the field and lit up the taco truck with their searchlights, Carlos began singing an aria from La Traviatta because it was the only aria he knew. He accompanied himself by plunking on an ancient one string guitar he'd found when he'd been shoved under the sink during their high speed chase earlier.

Jack ran to Constance and grabbed both leaf blowers, tossing one to Smokey as he ran back to him and they stationed themselves with the leaf blowers in a row of strawberries, turning them on. Largely because Smokey explained there is nothing unusual about gardeners in Oxnard doing their work in the

343

middle of the night.

Once the awning was secure, the nephews ran to Constance and grabbed the three remaining mop handles and joined their uncle, who pretended to be diligently poking things among the strawberries, like any good field worker would do with headless mop handles. In the middle of the night.

As Suzanne lit the glass devotional candles she found beneath the dashboard of the taco truck, Constance ran up, grabbed her hand and pulled her into her arms, whispering in her ear.

"Dance."

Fung Wah and the Three wiped tears away as it occurred to them they were the first to be witnessing the Dance of the Wu in three millennia.

Officer Martinez was the first on the scene, and what he saw made him wonder what his wife had put in his coffee. While field workers toiled in the dark with only the moonlight to see by, two gardeners with leaf blowers appeared to be landscaping the strawberry field while people sat eating whole avocados and heads of iceberg lettuce with what looked like stale day-old tortillas.

Meanwhile a man was plunking a single guitar string and singing some opera song while two women in a passionate embrace danced in the moonlight. None of them had a drop of blood on them, but there were bloody bodies all over the field. Lots of them.

"What the hell is going on here?" Constance turned to the confused officer and smiled the Wu's trademark smile of serenity.

"What does it look like? It's a wedding reception. See?"

Constance Void held Suzanne's hand up to the floodlight to show him the wedding ring. She kissed the warrior therapist's cheek and then pointed to the far side of the field near where Fung Wah and the Three pretended to be doing back breaking work not far from the GWEN tower.

"And that over there is our wedding cake. It's chocolate."

As the other officers approached, their shoulder mounted radios crackling, Officer Martinez looked to where she was pointing. The GWEN tower had been defaced yet again with chocolate pudding and toilet paper, only this time they'd caught the culprits.

But Constance patiently explained that it had been that previous act of culinary art that had inspired them to have their reception in Oxnard Plains so they could turn the tower into their own testament to love.

"Think of it," Suzanne said, clearly improvising. "Our act of devotion to each other will be broadcast all over the world in the frequency of love."

Haj joined in with some important culinary facts about unusual wedding cakes throughout history, and improvised a bit himself when he claimed to have provided the pudding.

Constance Void was relieved the midgets had taken all the little plastic pudding cups with them when they left, blaming their munchies on the Rastafarians.

It wouldn't have been prudent for the Muslim to be caught lying to the authorities. Or any Muslim, for that matter. That's something that's better left up to the professionals, like bankers and Wall Street brokers and CEOs, who are more experienced at lying to authorities without suffering any consequences whatsoever.

"What about all the bodies in the field?" Officer Martinez demanded.

They all shrugged their shoulders at the same time.

"We just thought whoever owns the field had put out gopher traps. We're from the suburbs. What do we know about agriculture?"

"Besides, it's dark out. Hard to tell the difference between a dead gopher and a possibly dead or maybe just mortally wounded mercenary gangster from Orange County."

Toole could always be counted on to be the voice of reason. In fact if one were to look up the definition of the word *reason,* it would show as an example a man biting into a head of iceberg lettuce outside a taco truck at three in the morning in an Oxnard strawberry field full of dead or maybe just mortally wounded corporate mercenary gangsters from Orange County.

The officers were not willing to accept any of what they were being told that morning until Ventura County Superior Court Bailiff Roz Ferriday stepped out of the taco truck.

How many times had Roz worked their appearance to testify in a case into their own schedule so they wouldn't lose a day's work, getting them in and out of the courthouse and back to work in record time?

How many times had she conveniently hit the *delete* button on the court's computer and made their own parking tickets or traffic fines disappear? The pretty officer of the court had eliminated enough of their personal debt to society for them to know they owed her. Big time. Even if it meant swearing to secrecy the fact that there appeared to have been witnesses to the Battle of Strawberry Fields, but they got away in a taco truck.

Which explains why so much legend has understandably sprung up about who was and who was not at the battle. The official record was suppressed for the same reason official records always are: somebody paid to make the truth disappear.

Only in this case, Roz paid it forward and waited for the truth to appear so she could then make it disappear. After everyone had finished eating their heads of lettuce, of course.

Toole and Roz drove the Sebring as the curious

347

cast of characters piled back into the taco truck. Lumbering back to the service road they had taken when they got off the 101, Constance paused. She had no idea where they were going. Left, back into Oxnard? Or right, back onto the freeway? Fung Wah told her to go left.

Of course Roz wanted to know where they were going, considering her apartment was too small to take all of them there, and heaved a sigh of relief that she was behind them in Toole's car so couldn't give them the address.

"Head toward the Marina. There's a boat that will take us to our ship." Fung Wah spoke with the confidence of a man who had prepared his entire life for this moment. Blade's heart sank when he realized the little pouch of aphrodisiac in his pocket really was the last he'd be getting from the herbalist.

Toole knew there was a lot he needed to think about before knowing what to tell Roz and what not to. He also knew if he were to file a report at work with the details of what had really happened, including who and what Constance Void actually was, the NSA would jump on the bandwagon along with the CIA and the Waltons.

Isn't it just like corporations and their playmates to want to kill anything that threatens profits? Or maybe the NSA might even decide they were just as eager to reverse engineer the magic of the

Wu as the Chinese, now that their new facility in Utah was up and running and they had so much more storage space.

But Toole knew the magic of the Wu was really not all that different from the technology that the governments of the world and their corporate masters, including his own, had already developed and been using for anything but the benefit of their own people. He remembered the words of his mother's favorite science fiction writer about any sufficiently advanced technology being indistinguishable from magic.

Wasn't it about time for the people to have some magic of their own, magic that wasn't fueled by the military industrial complex, that wasn't corporate owned? But Roz interrupted his thoughts and he realized he wouldn't mind her doing that for the rest of his life.

"I had begun to suspect there was something unusual going on, something cosmic at work when those stoner riffs she was giving me contained the exact same images I had seen in my dreams the night before. It was in those same dreams I was told to start knitting the caps and use copper thread in them. Something was up, Toole, and I knew it. Are you following me?"

Toole nodded, beginning to feel himself melt into the sound of her voice. It was a feeling he wanted to spend a lifetime getting to know. Roz was beyond a breath of fresh air; she was more like the air itself.

"First I dreamed I needed to call my knit caps the Ferriday Cap. Then the Void started showing up in my courtroom at the same time I started getting those cups of pudding on my desk. It was all connected. I knew it was, but I didn't know how or why.

All I knew was the Void was involved, and something was telling me to create these knit caps in the bright colors of the Rastafarians and start taking them down to Venice Beach."

"Do you believe in synchronicity?" She searched Toole's eyes with a look that broke his heart and then knit it back together again so it was stronger than he had ever dreamed it could be.

Toole believed in synthetic synchronicity. He wanted more than anything to lie, to tell her those meaningful coincidences were arranged by some mystical force that we might never know or fully understand.

But he had been with the NSA too long, had seen the way technology that is indistinguishable from magic had been used to create events that looked to the naked eye like synchronicity.

In fact, the intelligence industry was eternally grateful to Carl Jung for coining the term, because by the time he did our scientists were already hard at work creating a synthetic version of it for their corporate friends. They just didn't have a name for it.

But these weren't the things he wanted to tell her. He wanted a new way of looking at the world now she was by his side. He looked at his Roz of the halo eyes and the words of Constance Void came to him. He smiled and reached for her hand.

"I believe in celebrating the random."

For the second time that night the taco truck found itself on Channel Islands Boulevard as it neared the Oxnard Marina. As Constance steered the truck in that direction Fung Wah told her to park as close to the harbor docks as possible.

Since it was a food truck, it only made sense to park it right in front of the Cod Almighty Restaurant on the dock. It would be at least another three hours before any delivery trucks showed up, and since it was Sunday even that was unlikely. The atheists who owned it liked to take Sundays off to have fun while the fundamentalists were dressing up like waxed fruit and sitting on wooden benches having their intellects polished to match.

Toole pulled in behind the taco truck feeling pretty good about all of them getting through the battle safely and having Roz by his side. And that was when it happened. The kind of thing nobody ever sees coming, especially when they've let down their guard and relaxed.

Without warning, unseen by any of them until it was too late, the sixteen badly behaved Jewish midgets came out of nowhere and T-Boned the taco truck. Nobody could possibly have prepared for it, and everyone in the van could have been in grave danger of being forced through fifteen excruciating minutes of the midgets explaining their evil endgame.

But because they were midgets nobody felt a thing when they slammed into the taco truck at full speed. Have you ever seen a midget run? They aren't gazelles. You really should know that if you're planning on getting midgets to do any T-Boning for you. They really don't run very fast.

The impact was felt by no one – if by impact you mean the barely discernible little bit of force created by a herd of sixteen stampeding badly behaved Jewish midgets almost bouncing off a taco truck. In fact, nobody even knew they were there until Toole opened the car door and looked down, and by then the Rastafarians were taking care of it.

Although the Rastafarians had persuaded the midgets to turn over a new leaf, they hadn't been able to resist the temptation to have one last hurrah.

It could have been much worse, when you consider what they'd been exposed to earlier that night and how suggestible midgets can be, especially badly behaved Jewish midgets. But only sixteen specific badly behaved Jewish midgets. The others are probably perfectly nice people. We really must support them in their efforts to understand why they are so badly behaved.

The cast of characters previously known as patients of the Pleasant Valley Sunday Rehabilitation and Psychiatric Treatment Center in Camarillo poured out of the back of the taco truck, followed by Fung Wah and his nephews Dick Cheney and Bill O'Reilly. Pat Robertson and Smokey Methson had squeezed into the truck's kitchen pantry cupboard and were having trouble untangling themselves. Like all young lovers who are convinced they are about to say goodbye to each other, they weren't too serious about the untangling.

"Why am I seeing funeral faces?"

The Wu had told Glenn and Haj, Jerry and Carlos, and of course Jack Kerouac back at the clinic that she would be leaving with the dawn when they were all discussing their plans for escaping Dr. Carlson's lunacy.

Even though she had no idea where she was going, she knew this chapter was coming to an end and it was almost time to put down the book and live the story. It was only fair she tell them she would be leaving. But none of them really knew what would come after that.

Where would they go? What would they do? What's worse, none of them knew what they would do without the Void.

"I am the Wu. You are never without me. Keep

working on your wireless connections, and don't forget to wear your Ferriday Caps until we get all the shenanigans taken care of. You already know the magic. It's in you.

But if you need to speak with me, log on and connect. Especially if it has to do with pudding. You'll find me. And if all else fails, climb Wu Mountain and sit in a cave with me. I'll be busy channeling Milarepa so I can kick his ass for being such an unobtainable role model."

Carlos laughed despite himself and wiped a tear away. So did Jerry, after he quickly did a search to find out who Milarepa was.

Jack Kerouac was beaming the way only an alcoholic writer reborn in sobriety can, especially when they've had that epiphany that leads them to their first bestseller. Haj was the embodiment of pure bliss, but Glenn looked distraught and stood somewhat apart from everyone else, pointing at herself. Constance smiled gently and shook her head.

"Nonsense, Glenn. There is absolutely nothing about you that's corrupted. Don't you remember what Jerry found out when he did that search? You are no longer bound by the court to stay at the clinic. You're free to do what you are best at."

Sadly, Glenn had no idea what that was. Other than pointing at corruption and vanquishing evil she really wasn't good at anything else. She wasn't even good at combing her hair.

But the Void had spoken with Jerry who was quite skilled at website building and graphic art. He loved the idea of being a co-creator of a new animated web series about an unlikely superhero called The Point. Based on the events in the life of Glenn Greenworld, real life superhero.

Out of the mist that was beginning to rise off Channel Islands Harbor as the sun began to announce its intentions, they started to hear the low hum of an approaching craft. The midgets had helped the Rastafarians set up the kettle drums and as they played a Reggae cover of Hotel California each midget ceremoniously dropped his Izmail off the dock into the frigid Pacific water. Toole had heard of a men's acapella group that did a Reggae cover of it, and was relieved he didn't have to investigate to see if they wore robes.

He looked at the Void and realized it didn't bother him that she was a real live breathing person. It didn't even bother him that she was making eye contact with him. He still had so much to ask, so much to say.

He felt like he'd gotten to know the Void so well in the short time he'd known of her existence, while at the same time getting to know nothing about her at all. Had he not been in the process of becoming a paradox junkie, it would have been unsettling. Seeing the look on his face, Constance smiled.

"No time for goodbyes, Creepy Guy. You had to have known I wouldn't let you get away that easy."

Toole was mildly irritated that she was giving him the same platitudes that she'd given the others. That *you can find me if you need me* crap might work on them, but he was a horse of a different feather. What was worse, she still called him Creepy Guy.

"Why are you still calling me that?"

"Because you're a creep, Creepy Guy. Get over it, you freak. Besides, we'll have plenty of time for twenty questions on our trip. We can figure out what your name should be along the way. You really don't seem like a Toole anymore."

She was sensing he'd gotten lost in the conversation. Boys do that. Never send them into the forest of their minds without breadcrumbs. But if it's a cyber forest, better make it cookie crumbs.

"On our trip? What trip?"

Toole was beginning to feel the urge to tap his toe and pace a cubicle. Why was he always the last to hear about things?

"I got some smoke signals back there. Your mother wants to meet her future daughter in-law. So I sent some smoke signals of my own and am pretty confident I can persuade the captain to swing by Honduras so you three can spend some time together.

She says to bring extra moisturizer because she's out. I guess all that filtered air so deep underground really dries out the skin. She misses the salt sea air. But not the tar balls. Do either of you like nude beaches?"

She also hoped the captain wouldn't mind swinging by Seattle. She'd heard Puget Sound was nice in the spring and wanted to talk with Bill Nye. When asked in an interview on whether homosexuality makes sense in the context of evolution, his response had been that we should just celebrate being alive, that homosexuality is something that happens in nature and it didn't stop life from going on.

Since life itself in this universe is random, isn't Bill Nye actually saying celebrate the random? Constance Void hoped so, because men of science who celebrate the random are sexy. She hoped to tell him that in person. And then talk some sense into him about his refusal to acknowledge the universe's omniscience.

Never mind that a ship traveling from the east Pacific to China would not ordinarily go anywhere near either Honduras or Seattle. Like the Wu said, she is confident about the intel she was able to collect with the smoke signals and is sure it can be arranged. Confidence is really all the best kind of magic takes.

Toole was neither surprised to hear his mother was still alive nor reluctant to be leaving the American Deep State for one with better beaches.

And Roz wanted to object to the plans that involved her, but she was speechless. She couldn't think of a single reason not to get on board the little sloop that would motor sail them out to the ship.

"Oh wait," she said, suddenly thinking of the one thing that mattered. "What about the taco truck? And my apartment? "

Constance assured her Jerry and Glenn would take good care of the taco truck. Since both of them have valid driver's licenses, she didn't think there would be a problem with them taking over the job of driving it for her friend.

As for the apartment, they were both welcome to use it as a home base while starting over again and getting their new collaboration under way. Roz had always had a fondness for superheroes, especially female superheroes.

"Just promise to send the link when your first episode is up."

She handed Jerry the keys to both the taco truck and her apartment before disappearing down into the galley. Roz hated goodbyes, and she hated crying in front of people even more.

Jerry tossed the keys to Glenn and told her to drive. He wanted to dig through the kitchen for something to eat. That avocado and lettuce he'd had at the strawberry field was the first actual food he'd eaten in a long time, and all he could think about was having some more. A lot more.

Constance and Suzanne stood looking at each

other for a long time not saying a thing. They really didn't need to, did they? Suzanne knew what she would be doing, and thanks to Toole knew her car was still where she left it.

Once she'd gotten what she wanted out of her house, she would be taking up residence in the spare office at Pleasant Valley Sunday as the new personnel director.

And the first new hire she intended to make was an activities director. Someone with a wide range of knowledge who can replace the television in the day room with story-telling, poetry, yoga, music and exploration of other cultures around the world. In other words, the clinic and its patients needed a technician of the sacred.

Of course, the first person who came to mind for the position was Carlos, the pantheist who was no longer xenophobic. She knew the first time she set foot in the clinic that's where she wanted to be permanently.

And there was that moment she had with Dr. Carlson. Someone had to keep an eye on that lunatic, and she was just the woman to do it. She already had him thinking he had her wrapped around his finger. Plus, she was certain Constance Void would see to it the man began receiving smoke signals regularly. Suzanne was confident she was just the person to help him translate them.

Toole tossed his keys to Haj and told him to drive

Suzanne back to her car in the parking lot of the Camarillo Ralph's and leave the Sebring where her car had been. The NSA could figure it out from there. Since they don't have field agents, it would probably take some time, and he really didn't care.

The ride would give Suzanne the opportunity to talk to Haj about the second position she needed to fill. The clinic needed someone with knowledge about both nutrition and culinary arts. Someone who can acquire locally grown produce from farmers who don't use chemicals or put wax on any of it. Someone who understands the first place to turn for healing the mind and body isn't the pharmacy, it's the farmacy.

As the sloop pulled away from the dock, Fung Wah waved goodbye and so did his nephews, who had removed their American names and left them in a steaming heap on the dock. They could find no redeeming qualities in Bill O'Reilly, Dick Cheney, or Pat Robertson and definitely didn't want to bring any of what they stood for to a place of purity and magical beauty like Wu Mountain.

Smokey hadn't wanted to say anything when his beloved was carrying that awful name around, but he was relieved he'd left it behind. He could see those names doing nothing but weighing all of them down. And he fully understood how unencumbered the Three needed to be to successfully bring the Wu.

In fact, when he was invited to join them on Wu

Mountain, the first thing he did was start asking them about the wonderful new Chinese name they were going to help him find.

Blade stood watching the sloop disappear down the harbor and knew he'd made the right decision when he chose to stay, even though going home to China with them was tempting. But he felt he could do so much more for the greater good by staying in America, despite the potential danger.

He would tell his employers that he'd gone to the strawberry fields to try to recover the Wu as soon as he realized the full scope of her powers and it dawned on him for the first time it all wasn't just a fairy tale. And because he'd been there, he was now able to identify the high ranking American military official who was a double agent working for Mossad.

As is often the case when a man becomes enamored of his powers, the admiral lost them. And without them, he was defenseless against the inevitable shenanigans that were to follow. Admiral Thumbsen would be a very valuable asset to the Chinese. Very valuable indeed.

The morning sun was bouncing off the water and dancing in Roz's halo eyes as they watched Oxnard Shores disappear through the porthole.

"Speaking of names, did your mother seriously not give you a first name?"

He wanted to blush. He wanted to change the

subject. He wanted to do all the things he'd done his entire life to avoid telling someone what his first name was. But those halo eyes wrapped themselves around him, making him feel safer than he'd ever felt in his life. More than anything he wanted her to know everything there was to know about him and more.

"Shuman. My first name is Shuman."

ABOUT THE AUTHOR

Adrienne Veronese grew up in the Pacific Northwest, attending the University of Oregon and Antioch University West in Seattle. She is the author of Indigo Guardian, Tales of a Drunken Shopping Cart, and The Good, the Bad & the Secret Squirrel.

Adrienne lives and writes on Northern California's Redwood Coast.